CUTTING EDGE

NEW EDITION

STARTER   **WORKBOOK**

T0346209

SARAH CUNNINGHAM
PETER MOOR CHRIS REDSTON AND FRANCES MARNIE

CONTENTS

Grammar focus 1

Names and introductions: *I* and *you*; *my* and *your*

1a Complete the sentences with *I* and *you*; *my* and *your*.

1 Hello, ___*I*___ 'm Roy Magee.

3 Hello. What's _____ name?

2 Are _____ Teresa Daley?

4 **A:** Hello, _____ name's Frank.
   B: Hi, _____ 'm Paola. Nice to meet _____ .

b 🎧 **1.1 Listen and check.**

2a Put the words in the correct order to complete the conversations.

Conversation 1
A: Nina. / Hello, / I'm
  Hello, I'm Nina.
B: Nina. / Florian. / My / Hi, / name's

_____

Conversation 2
A: Judith? / you / Are

_____

B: right. / that's / Yes,

_____

Conversation 3
A: Simon. / name? / Hello, / What's / I'm / your

_____

B: Jonathan. / Nice / My / meet / name's / you. / to

_____

b 🎧 **1.2 Listen and check.**

Pronunciation

Names and introductions: *I* and *you*; *my* and *your*

3 🎧 **1.3** Listen to the sentences. Circle the word you hear.

1	I	(my)	you	your
2	I	my	you	your
3	I	my	you	your
4	I	my	you	your
5	I	my	you	your
6	I	my	you	your

Vocabulary

Jobs

4 Use the photo clues to complete the crossword with the missing words.

Pronunciation

Jobs

5 🎧 **1.4** Listen and put the words in the correct column.

accountant   ~~actor~~   assistant   business
engineer   police   teacher   waiter

●•	•●	•●•	••●
actor			

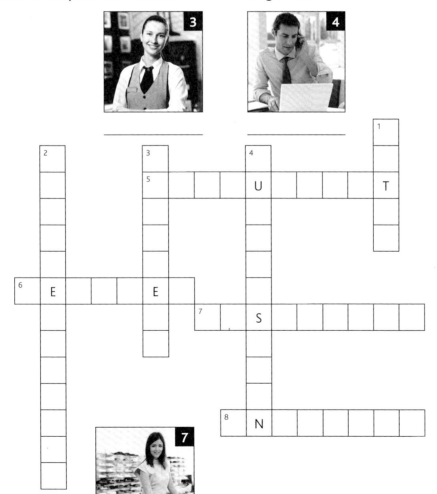

Shop

Grammar focus 2
a/an with jobs

6 Write *a* or *an* and the correct job.

1

I'm Adam. I'm <u>a doctor</u>.

2

I'm Anna. I'm __ _____ .

3

A: Are you a shop assistant?
B: No, I'm __ _____ .

4

A: What's your job?
B: I'm __ _____ .

5

A: Are you __ _____?
B: Yes, that's right.

6

A: Are you __ _____?
B: Yes, I am.

Vocabulary
The alphabet and *How do you spell ... ?*

7 🎧 **1.5 Listen and complete the names of the famous people.**

1

<u>C</u> A T <u>HE</u> R I N E   Z E T <u>A</u> - J O N <u>ES</u>

2

_ U _ I _ T   _ I _ O _ _ E

3

_ U E _ T _ N   T _ R _ N _ I N _

4

_ E _ _ N   S _ _ C _ Y

6

Numbers 0–20

8a Write the numbers.

three	_3_	ten	_____
six	_____	seventeen	_____
eleven	_____	four	_____
eighteen	_____	twelve	_____
nine	_____	five	_____

b Spell the numbers.

1	_one_	16	_____
7	_____	14	_____
8	_____	20	_____
13	_____	15	_____
2	_____	19	_____

Listen and read
Personal information

9a 🎧 **1.6** Listen to and/or read the texts.

What is
1 Sophia's job? _____
2 Tony's job? _____

Hello. My name's Sophia and my surname is Spencer. It's spelt S-P-E-N-C-E-R. I'm an actor. My email address is sspencer@yahoo.com.

Hi. My name's Tony. My family name is Banbury. That's B-A-N-B-U-R-Y. My phone number is 07963 241856. I'm an engineer.

b Listen to and/or read the texts again and answer the questions.

1 How do you spell Sophia's surname?

_____

2 What's Sophia's email address?

_____

3 What's Tony's phone number?

_____

4 How do you spell Tony's family name?

_____

Language Live
Hello and goodbye

10a Underline the correct word.

Mala: Hello, [1]**My / I'm** Mala. What's your name?
Lorenzo: Hi, Mala. [2]**My / I'm** name's Lorenzo. Nice to meet you.
Mala: Nice to meet [3]**you / your**, too. How do you spell [4]**you / your** name?
Lorenzo: L – O – R – E – N – Z – O.
Mala: Lorenzo, this [5]**is / are** Louis.
Lorenzo: Hi, Louis. Nice to [6]**meet / see** you.
Mala: Goodbye, Lorenzo. [7]**Meet / See** you again.
Lorenzo: Goodbye, Mala.

b 🎧 **1.7** Listen and check.

Pronunciation
/aɪ/

11 🎧 **1.8** Listen and say these words.

1 I	3 Hi!	5 nice
2 I'm	4 fine	6 my

Writing
Sentences and questions

12 Write ? or . in the circles.

1 'What's your name ⑦'
  'My name's Natalia ⦿'
2 'Are you Anna Schmidt ◯'
  'No, I'm Barbara Schmidt ◯'
3 'Hi, Sonja! How are you ◯'
  'I'm fine ◯ And you ◯'
4 'What's your family name ◯'
5 'My phone number is 07456 345345 ◯'
6 'What's your job ◯'
  'I'm a singer ◯'

13 Write the sentences with capital letters.

_H T_   _I S_   _N_
1 hi tony, i'm salvatore. nice to meet you.
2 **A:** 'are you Harry?'
  B: 'no, I'm Jim.'
3 **A:** 'what's your job? are you an actor?'
  B: 'no, i'm a singer.'
4 **A:** 'what's your name?'
  B: 'my name's andrea.'
5 **A:** 'hello, abdul, how are you?'
  B: 'i'm fine.'
6 my name's istvan and i'm an engineer.

Vocabulary

Countries

1 Write the name of the country.

1

N A G E L N D   *England*

2

A B R I L Z   B_____

3

N A J A P   J_____

4

Y A T I L   I_____

5

A U S   The U_____

6

T L I A A U R S A   A_____

7

M V T N A I E   V_____

8

E P T Y G   E_____

9

N I C H A   C_____

10

I S A S U R   R_____

Grammar focus 1
be with *I* and *you*

2a Put the words in the correct order.

Adam: name's / Hello. / Adam. / My
1 *Hello. My name's Adam.*

Francesca: Francesca. / I'm / you. / Nice / to meet
2 *I'm* _____ .

Adam: are / from? / you / Where
3 _____ ?

Francesca: Italy. / from / I'm
4 _____ .

Adam: Rome? / you / Are / from
5 _____ ?

Francesca: I'm / Milan. / No, / from
6 _____ .

Francesca: you / student? / a / Are
7 _____ ?

Adam: I'm / teacher. / No, / your
8 _____ .

b 🎧 2.1 Listen and check.

3 Make the sentences negative.

1 I'm from the United States.
 I'm not from the United States.
2 You're from London.
 _____
3 You're a teacher.
 _____
4 I'm a teacher.
 _____
5 I'm from a big country.
 _____
6 You're from Russia.
 _____

Grammar focus 2
be with *he, she* and *it*

4 🎧 2.2 Listen. Are these sentences true (T) or false (F)?

1 Miles is a waiter.   *F*
2 Bruno is from Brazil.   ___
3 Paula is from Italy.   ___
4 Yasmin is a teacher.   ___
5 Her name is Mary.   ___
6 Hanoi is in Vietnam.   ___
7 His name is Giles.   ___
8 Perth is in Australia.   ___

5 Circle the correct alternative to complete the sentences.

1 A: *Is* / *Are* your teacher from England?
  B: Yes, she *be* / *is*.
2 A: Where *is* / *are* Boston?
  B: *It's* / *She's* in the USA.
3 A: Where *is* / *be* Carlos from?
  B: *It's* / *He's* from Spain.
4 A: *Is* / *Be* Manchester in the USA?
  B: No, it *not* / *isn't*. It's in England.
5 A: *Is* / *Are* David a student?
  B: Yes, *he is* / *he's*.
6 A: *Is* / *Are* Ahmid from Morocco?
  B: No, he *is* / *isn't*.

Vocabulary
Countries and nationalities

6a Complete the sentences.

1 He's from Britain. He's _British_ .
2 She's from the United States. She's _____ .
3 He's from Japan. He's _____ .
4 She's from China. She's _____ .
5 He's from Brazil. He's _____ .
6 She's from Portugal. She's _____ .
7 She's from Egypt. She's _____ .
8 He's from Argentina. He's _____ .

b 🎧 2.3 Listen and check.

Pronunciation
Nationalities

7a Count the syllables in these words.

	2 Syllables	3 Syllables	4 Syllables
British			
Japanese			
Brazilian			
Portuguese			
Egyptian			
Russian			
Spanish			
Polish			

b Put the nationalities from 7a in the correct columns.

●•	••●	•●•	•●••
British			

Grammar focus 3
his/her

8 Circle the correct answer.

1 _____ name is Ahmet.
   a (His)   b He   c He's
2 What's _____ name?
   a she's   b she   c her
3 Where is _____ from?
   a she   b her   c she's
4 What's _____ job? She's a student.
   a her   b his   c you
5 Is _____ name Diana?
   a she   b her   c she's
6 _____ name's Franco. He's a footballer.
   a His   b Her   c He's

Pronunciation
his/her

9 🎧 2.4 Listen to the sentences. Circle the word you hear.

1 (She's)   He's   5 She's   He's
2 Her   His   6 She's   He's
3 he's   his   7 she   he
4 Her   His   8 her   his

Vocabulary
Numbers (21–100) and How old ... ?

10 Underline the correct answer.

1 11 + 11 = twelve   twenty-two   thirty-two
2 86 – 63 = twenty-three   thirty-three   forty-three
3 8 x 8 = forty-eight   fifty-six   sixty-four
4 100 – 11 = seventy-nine   eighty-nine   ninety-nine
5 9 x 3 = seventeen   twenty-seven   thirty-seven
6 36 + 22 = fifty-two   fifty-six   fifty-eight
7 13 x 6 = seventy-two   seventy-eight   eighty-four
8 30 x 3 = sixty   eighty   ninety

11 Look at the pictures and complete the questions.

1 How old is Ricky?
   He's 26.
   Where's he from?
   He's from Australia.
   He's Australian.

Ricky Wood
26
Sydney,
Australia

2 _____ Jarek?
   He's 20.
   _____ ?
   He's from Poland.
   He's Polish.

Jarek Zmuc
20
Warsaw,
Poland

3 _____ Ayse?
   She's 17.
   _____ ?
   She's from Turkey.
   She's Turkish.

Ayse Sükür
17
Ankara,
Turkey

4 _____ Betty?
   She's 41.
   _____ ?
   She's from Brazil.
   She's Brazilian.

Betty Fern
41
São Paulo,
Brazil

Listen and read

Where in the world ... ?

12a Match the places in the box with pictures 1–6.

Machu Picchu   New South Wales
Taj Mahal   UAE   UK   Yale

1 _____Yale_____
2 _____
3 _____
4 _____
5 _____
6 _____

b 🎧 **2.5 Listen to and/or read about these places.**

c (Circle) the correct answer.

1 Yale is a university. It is in the
  a UK.   **b** USA.   **c** UAE.
2 Agra is a city. It is in
  a England.   **b** Australia.   **c** India.
3 Sydney is the capital of
  a New South Wales. **b** Scotland. **c** Wales.
4 The Taj Mahal is
  a 200 years old. **b** 400 years old. **c** 600 years old.
5 Machu Picchu is
  a a university. **b** a city.   **c** a country.
6 Abu Dhabi is the capital of the
  a UK.   **b** USA.   **c** UAE.

d Complete the questions with *What* or *Where*.

1 _*What*_ is Yale? It's a university.
2 _____ is Yale? It's in the United States of America.
3 _____ is Machu Picchu? It's in South America.
4 _____ is Machu Picchu? It's an old city.
5 _____ is Abu Dhabi? It's in the UAE.

Where in the world ... ?

What is Yale and where is it?

Yale is a university in the United States of America – the USA. It's in New Haven, Connecticut.

Where is New South Wales? Is it in Wales?

No! New South Wales isn't in Wales ... and it isn't in the United Kingdom. It's in Australia. The capital is Sydney.

What is the UK?

The UK is the United Kingdom – England, Scotland Wales and Northern Ireland. London is the capital city of the United Kingdom.

What is the UAE?

The UAE is the United Arab Emirates – seven countries in the Persian Gulf. The capital is Abu Dhabi.

What is Machu Picchu and where is it?

Machu Picchu is an old city in the Urabamba Valley in Peru, in South America.

Where is the Taj Mahal? How old is it?

The Taj Mahal is in Agra, a city in India. It's about 400 years old.

03 IN ANOTHER COUNTRY

Vocabulary
Plural nouns

1 Write the words.

1 a _man_

3 a _____

5 a _____

2 a _____

4 a _____

6 a _____

2 Write the plurals.

1	man	_men_	5	car	_____
2	woman	_____	6	bus	_____
3	child	_____	7	shop	_____
4	person	_____	8	country	_____

Pronunciation
Plural nouns

3 🎧 **3.1** Listen and circle the word you hear.

1 place   (places)
2 sandwich   sandwiches
3 student   students
4 nationality   nationalities
5 address   addresses
6 country   countries
7 child   children
8 person   people
9 woman   women
10 man   men

Grammar focus 1
this/that, these/those

4a Underline the correct alternative to complete the questions.

1 'Is **this** / **these** your pen?'
2 'Are **that** / **those** people from Japan?'
3 'Who's **that** / **those** in the café?' 'My teacher.'
4 'What are **this** / **these**?' 'I don't know.'
5 'Is **this** / **these** your car?' 'Yes, it is.'
6 'Who are **that** / **those** children over there?'
7 'Is **that** / **those** hotel expensive?' 'Yes, it is!'

b 🎧 **3.2** Listen and check. Practise saying the sentences aloud.

Vocabulary
Common adjectives

5a Complete the sentences with the opposite adjective.

    1   Is the shop expensive?   No, it's _cheap_ .
    2   Is he friendly?   No, he's very _____ .
    3   Is Ali happy?   No, he's _____ .
    4   Isn't this fantastic?   No, it's _____ .

  b 🎧 3.3 Listen and say the answers.

Listen and read
Places to eat in Newcastle

6a 🎧 3.4 Listen to and/or read about four restaurants in Newcastle. Which type of food from the box is not mentioned?

> Argentinian   Chinese   English   French
> Italian   Japanese

  b Which two restaurants does the writer like?

  c Read the statements and decide if they are true (T) or false (F).

    1   *The Sushiya* is a good restaurant.   _T_
    2   *Vaqueros* is in the city centre.   _____
    3   *The Chinatown* is expensive.   _____
    4   The waiters in *The Piccolo* are Italian.   _____
    5   The food in *The Sushiya* is really cheap.   _____
    6   The waiters in *The Chinatown* are friendly.   _____
    7   The waiters in *Vaqueros* aren't Argentinian.   _____
    8   The food in *The Piccolo* is fantastic.   _____
    9   *The Chinatown* is a Vietnamese restaurant.   _____
   10   The food in *The Piccolo* isn't cheap.   _____

Places to eat in Newcastle

The Sushiya is a Japanese restaurant. It's in the city centre. The food is fantastic but it isn't cheap. The waiters are very friendly. It's a great restaurant! ✪✪✪✪✪

The new Italian restaurant, *The Piccolo* is expensive and the food is awful. The waiters are English, not Italian. They are unfriendly. This is not my favourite restaurant! ✪

The Argentinian restaurant, *Vaqueros*, isn't in the city centre but it is cheap and the food is great. The waiters are from Buenos Aires and very friendly. I like it! ✪✪✪✪

The Chinatown is a Chinese restaurant. It is cheap but the food isn't fantastic. The waiters are friendly. ✪✪

Grammar focus 2
be with *we* and *they*

7 Complete the sentences with *we*, *they*, *are* or *aren't*.

1 Their names __are__ Peter and Lynn. __They__ 're from Australia.
2 Mr and Mrs Palmer _____ in Room 838 – _____ 're in Room 836.
3 '_____ you from the United States?' 'No, _____ 're from Canada.'
4 No, we _____ happy with our hotel: it's very cold and it's expensive.
5 Eva and I _____ Czech – _____ 're from Prague.
6 Buses _____ expensive in my city – _____ 're very cheap.
7 Córdoba and Mendoza _____ big cities in Argentina.
8 'Is your hotel nice?' 'Yes, _____ 're very happy with it.'

8 Are these sentences correct (✓) or incorrect (✗)? Rewrite the incorrect sentences.

1 My name's Marta. [✓] _____
2 I are with my friends, Anna and Miguel. [✗] 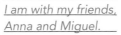 *I am with my friends,*  *Anna and Miguel.*
3 We is Spanish. [ ] _____
4 We are in London for a conference. [ ] _____
5 The conference are very interesting. [ ] _____
6 Our hotel are very comfortable. [ ] _____
7 The rooms is very large. [ ] _____
8 The food aren't very good. [ ] _____
9 The people in London are very friendly. [ ] _____
10 We is very happy. [ ] _____

9 <u>Underline</u> the correct answers.

We ¹**is** / **are** in Mexico City and it ²**is** / **are** fantastic! Our friends, Fred and Zoe, ³**is** / **are** also here. Our hotel ⁴**is** / **are** very good but expensive. Fred and Zoe ⁵**is** / **are** in an awful hotel but it ⁶**is** / **are** cheap. They ⁷**isn't** / **aren't** happy with the hotel. The restaurant in the hotel ⁸**isn't** / **aren't** Mexican – the food ⁹**isn't** / **aren't** great and the waiters ¹⁰**isn't** / **aren't** friendly. Our hotel ¹¹**is** / **are** the opposite! The Mexican food ¹²**is** / **are** very good, the people ¹³**is** / **are** very friendly and we ¹⁴**is** / **are** very happy.

Vocabulary
Food and drink

10 Find a food or drink word in each line.

1	D	G	F	C	R	I	C	E	G	T	U	Y
2	B	T	T	E	S	E	G	G	S	E	W	N
3	S	C	H	E	E	S	E	A	E	T	P	Y
4	T	E	N	L	P	E	M	R	M	E	A	T
5	A	E	V	E	G	E	T	A	B	L	E	S
6	N	M	D	F	T	B	R	E	A	D	H	T
7	S	N	B	T	F	I	S	H	B	R	S	J
8	A	C	O	F	F	E	E	C	R	I	G	O
9	N	R	L	E	L	R	W	M	I	L	K	W
10	Y	S	H	G	H	W	A	T	E	R	H	T
11	M	N	S	G	T	S	I	P	A	S	T	A
12	I	I	A	D	F	R	U	I	T	P	K	W

Language Live
In a café

11a Put the sentences and questions in the correct order.

1 have / Can / coffee, / I / please ?
   Can I have coffee, please?

2 me, / please. / for / Eggs
   _____

3 sandwich, / I / a / please? / Can / have
   _____

4 for / please. / The / me, / same
   _____

5 I / please? / the / Can / have / bill,
   _____

b 🎧 **3.5** Listen and check.

12a 🎧 **3.6** Listen and put the conversation in the correct order.

1 And for you, sir? ___
2 And to drink? ___
3 Yes, please? _1_
4 Orange _____ for me, please. ___
5 Can I have a ham _sandwich_, please? ___
6 No, _____ you. ___
7 Fish for me, _____ . ___
8 Anything else? ___
9 Can I have coffee, please? Black _____ . ___

b **Listen again and complete the dialogue with the correct words from the box.**

coffee   juice   please
~~sandwich~~   thanks

Writing
Holiday messages

13 Complete the postcard with the words and phrases from the box.

cheap   ~~everybody~~   expensive   friendly   How   See you

Hello 1 _everybody_ !!
2 _____ are you?
3 _____ in Thailand on holiday.
The hotel is fantastic, but it's very
4 _____ ! — $450 a day!
We're by the pool now!
The food in the local restaurants
is very 5 _____ — meat and
rice with a drink is only $8. The
people are 6 _____, too.
7 _____ soon!

Christopher, Martha
and the children

Flat D, 128 Canterbury Road

Ashford,

Kent AS9 GHS

UK

Vocabulary
Places in a town

1 Write the missing letters.

1 B <u>A</u> N <u>K</u>

5 _ A _ P _ _ K

2 B _ S S _ _ P

6 S _ P _ R _ _ _ K _ T

3 R _ S T _ _ R _ _ T

7 _ Q _ A _ E

4 _ T _ T _ _ N

8 _ I _ E _ A

Pronunciation
Places in a town

2 🎧 **4.1** Listen and (circle) the correct stress pattern for each word.

1 café	●·	·●	
2 hotel	●·	·●	
3 shopping	●·	·●	
4 restaurant	●··	·●·	··●
5 cinema	●··	·●·	··●
6 station	●·	·●	

Grammar focus 1
Prepositions of place

3 Look at the map and read sentences 1–8 below. Are they correct (✓) or incorrect (✗)? Rewrite the incorrect sentences.

1 The café is in the park. ✓ _____

2 The bank is on the left of the supermarket. ✗ *The bank is on the right of the bus stop.*

3 The restaurant is in North Road. ☐ _____

4 The cinema is on the right of the restaurant. ☐ _____

5 The bus stop is on the left of the bank near the supermarket. ☐ _____

6 The cinema is in South Road near the station. ☐ _____

7 The station is in North Road. ☐ _____

8 The hotel is on the right of the station. ☐ _____

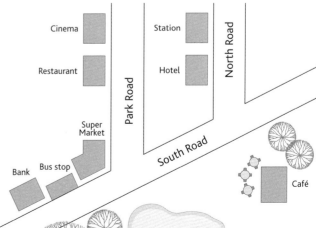

4a Underline the correct alternative to complete the sentences.
1 The bank's _in_ / _on_ the square.
2 'Where's the station?' 'It's _in_ / _on_ the left.'
3 The restaurant's on _right_ / _the right_.
4 Is your hotel near the _station_ / _the station_?
5 The cinema is on the left _of the restaurant_ / _the restaurant_.
6 Is the hotel _in_ / _at_ Station Road?
7 The cinema _isn't_ / _aren't_ in the square.
8 The hotel is on the left _to_ / _of_ the train station.

b 🎧 4.2 Listen and check. Practise saying the sentences aloud.

Grammar focus 2
there is and _there are_

5a Read the information about Crowley and complete the sentences with _there's_ or _there are_.

Crowley Town Guide

Hotel:	Hotel Europe (**), Park Street
Restaurants:	Il Buongustaio (Italian), Church Street
	Jasmine Peking (Chinese), St. Michael's Street
	The Crab & Lobster (Fish), Marton Street
Cafés:	The Pear Tree, Church Street
	Frederick's, Bridge Street
	Market Café, Market Square
Supermarket:	Tesco, Marton Road
Cinema:	Odeon, Church Street
Car Parks:	St. Michael's Street, Camley Road.
Banks:	NatWest / Barclays, Market Square
Post Office:	Park Street

** = two star

1 _There's_ a hotel in Crowley.
2 _____ three restaurants.
3 _____ an Italian restaurant.
4 _____ three cafés.
5 _____ a supermarket in Marton Road.
6 _____ a cinema in Church Street.
7 _____ two car parks.
8 _____ two banks in Market Square: _NatWest_ and _Barclays_.
9 _____ a post office in Park Street.

b 🎧 4.3 Listen and check. Practise saying the sentences aloud.

6 Are these sentences correct (✓) or incorrect (✗)? Rewrite the incorrect sentences.

1 There is a cinema in my town. ✓

2 There is three banks in Station Road. ✗
   There are three banks in
   Station Road.

3 There is two hotels in George Street. ☐
   _____

4 There is a café in the supermarket. ☐
   _____

5 There is a bus stop near the train station. ☐
   _____

6 There are a big park near the cathedral. ☐
   _____

7 There are an Indian restaurant on the left of the hotel. ☐
   _____

8 There are four restaurants in Bank Street. ☐
   _____

9 There are a small shop near the bus stop. ☐
   _____

10 There are five cafés in the town square. ☐
   _____

Pronunciation
_th-_

7 🎧 4.4 Listen and repeat.
1 These apples are cheap.
2 Where are they?
3 That man is very friendly.
4 There are three women in the picture.
5 There's a cathedral in the city centre.
6 This restaurant is very expensive.
7 Are those shops good?
8 This is my favourite hotel.
9 There's a yellow taxi in the picture.
10 Those men are in a café.

17

Listen and read
The World Showcase

8a 🎧 **4.5** Listen to and/or read about *The World Showcase*. Which country is it in?

....

China   France   Japan   the United Kingdom   the USA

....

The World Showcase

The World Showcase is in DisneyWorld in Florida, USA. There are eleven pavilions at the beautiful World Showcase Lagoon – and all the pavilions are about a different country in the world.

In the Chinese pavilion, there are two Chinese restaurants. In the Moroccan pavilion, there's a real Moroccan market.

For France, there's the Eiffel Tower (a small one!) and there's a cinema.

In the Italian pavilion, there's an Italian restaurant – *Alfredo's* – with real Italian pasta!

And in the United Kingdom pavilion, there's a pub – *The Rose and Crown* – with English food and drinks.

In the Japanese pavilion, there's a Japanese garden and a big Japanese store* – *Mitsukoshi*.

* *store* in American English = *shop* in British English

b Listen to and/or read the text again and answer these questions about *The World Showcase*.

1 Where are the Chinese restaurants?
   In the Chinese pavilion.

2 Where is *Alfredo's* restaurant?
   _____

3 Where is the cinema?
   _____

4 Where is *The Rose and Crown* pub?
   _____

5 Where is the *Mitsukoshi* store?
   _____

6 Where is the market?
   _____

Grammar focus 3
there is and *there are*
– positive, negative and questions

9a Write negative sentences using the prompts in brackets.

1 (a ***** hotel)
   There isn't a five-star hotel.

2 (any Indian restaurants)
   _____

3 (a train station)
   _____

4 (any internet cafés)
   _____

5 (a library)
   _____

6 (any beaches)
   _____

b 🎧 **4.6** Listen and check. Practise saying the sentences aloud.

10a Write questions using the words in brackets.

1 (a park)
   Is there a park   ?

2 (any good shops)
   _____ ?

3 (a university)
   _____ ?

4 (a bus station)
   _____ ?

5 (any cheap bars)
   _____ ?

6 (a cinema)
   _____ ?

b 🎧 **4.7** Listen and check. Practise saying the sentences aloud.

11 Match the sentence halves.

1 There are — **a** any French students in my class.

2 There's a — **b** any good shops near here?

3 There isn't — **c** good supermarket.

4 There aren't — **d** a university in your town?

5 Is there — **e** a lot of students in my city.

6 Are there — **f** a restaurant here.

12 Complete the sentences with *some*, *any* or *a*.

1 There's __a__ beautiful park near my house.
2 There are _____ good restaurants in the town.
3 Are there _____ small children in your family?
4 Is there _____ cinema in this town?
5 There aren't _____ famous people in my family.
6 There isn't _____ car park at the university.
7 There's _____ bus stop in Hope Street.
8 There are _____ American students here.

Vocabulary
Natural features

13 Unscramble the words.

1 EAS   _SEA_
2 KELA   _____
3 LNDASI   _____
4 IRREV   _____
5 ECBHA   _____
6 UTNNAMIO   _____

Language live
Directions

14 Complete the conversation below with the correct word from the box.

bank   ~~Excuse~~   in   left   near   there   Where

A: ¹_Excuse_ me. Is ²_____ a ³_____ near here?
B: Yes, there is. There's one on the ⁴_____ of the supermarket
A: The supermarket? ⁵_____'s that?
B: It's ⁶_____ the town centre ⁷_____ the High Street.
A: Thanks very much.
B: You're welcome.

15 🎧 **4.8 Listen to the conversations. Are these sentences true (T) or false (F)?**

Conversation 1
1 The woman wants to go to a park.   _F_

Conversation 2
2 The man wants to go to the supermarket.   ____
3 The bank is on the left.   ____

Conversation 3
4 The man wants to go to a café.   ____
5 There is a café in Park Road.   ____

Conversation 4
6 The woman wants to go to the train station. ____
7 The name of the road is Station Road.   ____

Writing
Your town

16a Complete the table about Auckland, New Zealand with the correct word from the box.

café   centre   famous   shops   small
~~town~~   years

My town
The name of my ¹_town_ is Auckland. It's in New Zealand. It is ²_____ for its theatre in the city centre. It is 90 ³_____ old. The Auckland Domain is the name of a big park in the ⁴_____ the town. There are also lots of cafés. My favourite ⁵_____ is *The Coffee and Chat House*. There are lots of big ⁶_____ in Queen Street and in Ponsonby, near the centre, there are ⁷_____ shops.

b Use the notes below to write a paragraph about Bourges, France.

Town:	Bourges
Where:	centre of France
Famous:	beautiful, old cathedral (800 years old)
Shops:	small shops in centre
Supermarkets:	two, near centre
Park:	near the cathedral
Restaurants:	lots near the station
Favourite:	La Folie, a French restaurant

Vocabulary
Family

1 Label the family tree with the words from the box.

children   daughter   grandchildren   grandfather
grandmother   ~~grandparents~~   husband   parents
son   wife

1 _grandparents_

Elvira
2 _____

Hugo
3 _____

Antonio
4 _____

5 _____

Marta
6 _____

7 _____

8 _____

Javier
9 _____

Gloria
10 _____

Grammar focus 1
Possessive 's

2a Look at the family tree. Complete the sentences with the words from the box.

brother   grandchildren   grandparents
~~husband~~   parents   sister   son   wife

1 Antonio is Marta's _husband_ .
2 Marta is Antonio's _____ .
3 Their _____ 's name is Javier.
4 Javier is Gloria's _____ .
5 Gloria is Javier's _____ .
6 Antonio and Marta are Javier and Gloria's _____ .
7 Hugo and Elvira are Gloria and Javier's _____ .
8 Gloria and Javier are Hugo and Elvira's _____ .

b 🎧 5.1 Listen and check.

3 Write *'s* in the correct place.

1 Is that Paul's mother?
2 What's your sister name?
3 John brother is a footballer.
4 There's a party at Frank house!
5 'Is this your book?' 'No, it's Barbara.'
6 Jackie is Catherine sister.
7 Our dog name is Max.

4 Write *possessive* or *is* for each sentence.

1 My father**'s** name is Frederick.
   possessive _____
2 What**'s** her name?
   _is_ _____
3 He**'s** from Scotland.
   _____
4 Ana**'s** children are at school.
   _____
5 Claire**'s** husband is Spanish.
   _____
6 His name**'s** Tony.
   _____
7 Michael**'s** parents are on holiday.
   _____
8 Pablo**'s** a footballer from Chile.
   _____

Listen and read
Carla's family

5a 🎧 **5.2 Listen to and/or read the text. Is it about:**

1 a mother, father and daughter?
2 a mother, father and son?
3 a mother and her two children?

My name's Carla. My husband's name is Miguel. We have one child, Lotta. She's 18. We're from Spain but we don't live there now. We live in Ireland. I work in a college near Dublin. I teach Spanish. Miguel and Lotta work in an expensive hotel in the city centre. They study English in the evening. I don't study in the evening – I teach in the evening!
Miguel and Lotta go to work by bus because we live near the college, we don't live in the city centre. We don't live in a house. We have a big flat near a park – it's fantastic. We are very happy here.

b Listen to and/or read the text again. Are these statements true (T) or false (F)?

1 Carla and her family live in Ireland.   _T_
2 They come from Portugal.   ___
3 Carla works in a hotel.   ___
4 Miguel and Lotta work in a cheap hotel.   ___
5 The hotel is in the city centre.   ___
6 Miguel and Lotta study English in the morning.   ___
7 Carla doesn't study English.   ___
8 Miguel and Lotta go to work by bus.   ___
9 They live near a park.   ___
10 They are sad in Dublin.   ___

Grammar focus 2
Present simple (*I, you, we, they*)

6a Complete the sentences with the correct form of the verb in brackets. Make the sentence positive (+) or negative (-).

1	I _study_ English.	(*study* +)
2	I _don't study_ French.	(*study* -)
3	They _____ a big car.	(*have* +)
4	They _____ a small car.	(*have* -)
5	You _____ in an office.	(*work* +)
6	You _____ in a hotel.	(*work* -)
7	We _____ coffee.	(*like* +)
8	We _____ tea.	(*like* -)
9	I _____ to work by bus.	(*go* +)
10	I _____ to work by train.	(*go* -)
11	They _____ in Wales.	(*live* +)
12	They _____ in Germany.	(*live* -)

b 🎧 **5.3 Listen and check.**

7 Write *don't* in the correct place to make negative sentences.

  don't
1 We⁄have an expensive car.
2 I study French.
3 They work in the centre of town.
4 I have a brother.
5 We live in Poland.
6 Our children drink tea.

Vocabulary
Verbs with noun phrases

8a Write the correct verb from the box in the circle.

go   live   ~~study~~   have   work

1 (study) French
at university
in the evening

2 ( ) in a big city
with your family
in Poland

3 ( ) for a big company
with children
in the centre of town

4 ( ) three children
a good job
a lot of friends

5 ( ) to school
to work by bus
home for lunch

b Complete the text with the correct form of one of the verbs from exercise 8a.

John and Angie don't ¹_work_, they ²___ to university. They ³___ medicine. They are husband and wife. They ⁴___ in a big flat near the university and ⁵___ home for lunch every day. They don't ⁶___ children but they ⁷___ a cat!

Pronunciation
Negatives

9 🎧 5.4 Listen and say these negative sentences.

1 We don't work in an office.
2 They don't go to work by bus.
3 I don't like coffee.
4 You don't study French.
5 We don't have an expensive car.

Grammar focus 3
Present simple questions (*I, you, we, they*)

10a Write the questions for these answers. Use the words in brackets.

1 (you / live / house / flat)
Do you live in a house or a flat?
I live in a flat.

2 (you / study / German)
_____?
No, I don't. I study English!

3 (they / have / any children)
_____?
Yes, two. Their names are Tom and Anna.

4 (live / town / city)
_____?
I live in Fermo – it's a town in Italy.

5 (have / any pets)
_____?
No, I don't like animals.

6 (he / have / any brothers and sisters)
_____?
Yes, one brother. His name's Mark.

7 (like / Chinese food)
_____?
No, I don't. I like Japanese food.

8 (work / office)
_____?
Yes, I do. I'm an accountant.

9 (live / parents)
_____?
No, I don't. I live with a friend.

10 (Maria and Guiseppe / teach / Italian / Spanish)
_____?
They teach both – Italian and Spanish!

b 🎧 5.5 Listen and check. Repeat the questions.

11a Write the short answers.

1 Do you live in a house? ✓
2 Do you study Japanese? ✗
3 Do you have any sisters? ✓
4 Do you live in America? ✗
5 Do you like dogs? ✓
6 Do you have a dog? ✗

1 *Yes, I do.*
2 *No, I don't.*
3 _____
4 _____
5 _____
6 _____

b 🎧 5.6 Listen and check.
Repeat the answers.

Pronunciation
Weak forms

12 🎧 5.7 Listen and repeat.

1 Do you study French?
2 Do you study at home?
3 Do you live alone?
4 Do you live in a house?
5 Who do you live with?
6 Where do you work?
7 Do you have any children?
8 Do you go to work by car?

Writing
A personal profile

13a <u>Underline</u> the correct words to complete each sentence in Donna's personal profile.

Hi, my ¹***name's*** / *names* Donna and I ²*'m* / *'ve* 18 years old. I'm ³***live*** / *from* Ireland. I ⁴*'m* / *I* a student.

I live ⁵*at* / ***with*** my parents in a nice flat in Dublin. I ⁶***don't*** / *'m not* have a big family: just Mum, Dad, me and ⁷***my*** / *your* brother. My parents' names ⁸*is* / ***are*** Declan and Rosemary. ⁹***They're*** / *They work* teachers. My ¹⁰*brother* / ***brother's*** name is Ciaran. We also have two cats: ¹¹*his* / ***their*** names are Benny and Bjorn.

I have three ¹²*grandfathers* / ***grandparents***: two grandfathers and one grandmother. My grandmother's ¹³***name*** / *names* is Iris, and ¹⁴***she is*** / *they are* 71 years old.

b Write five sentences about how your life is different from Donna's.

I'm not 18 years old, I'm 26 years old.

_____
_____
_____
_____
_____
_____
_____
_____
_____
_____

Vocabulary
Activities – verbs

1 Write the words.

1 People read   K O B O S   b _ooks_
              G M I Z N E A A S   m _agazines_
2 People play   M E G A S   g _____
              N I N S T E   t _____
3 People watch   M L I F S   f _____
4 People use   R E M O P C U T S   c _____
              L T O S P P A   l _____
5 People cook   N E D N I R   d _____
6 People listen to   M U C S I   m _____

Grammar focus 1
Present simple (*he, she, it*)

2 Complete the sentences with the *he, she* or *it* form of the verb in brackets.

1 My father really _likes_ football.   (*like*)
2 Patricia _____ the Internet at work.   (*use*)
3 Our daughter _____ a lot of television.   (*watch*)
4 I go to work by bus. It _____ at 8 a.m.   (*come*)
5 My father _____ the newspaper at work.   (*read*)
6 Danielle is a teacher. She _____ French.   (*teach*)
7 My friend Bob _____ in the United States.   (*live*)
8 David is a footballer. He _____ for Manchester United.   (*play*)
9 My town's nice – it _____ a cinema and a lot of cafés.   (*have*)

3 Rewrite these sentences as negatives.

1 My dog likes cats.
   My dog doesn't like cats.
2 Paul teaches English.
   _____
3 Carla lives with her parents.
   _____
4 My father likes rock music.
   _____
5 Sam plays tennis.
   _____
6 Olga works for a British company.
   _____
7 My country has a Disneyland.
   _____
8 Jenny likes football.
   _____

4a Read about Josh and Daniel.

> Josh and Daniel are good friends. They live in a flat in New York, but they are very different. Josh is 25 and studies at a business school. He goes to the gym every day and likes going out with his friends at the weekend.
>
> Daniel is 27 and is a businessman. He works a lot so he doesn't have much free time. He likes going to restaurants, but doesn't like cooking. He plays guitar and likes listening to live music. He reads a lot of magazines.

b Are these sentences about Josh or Daniel?

1 He is 25.   _Josh_
2 He works in an office.   _____
3 He eats in restaurants a lot.   _____
4 He goes to the gym everyday.   _____
5 He listens to live music.   _____
6 He plays a musical instrument.   _____
7 He is a student.   _____
8 He studies business.   _____
9 He doesn't like cooking.   _____
10 He reads magazines.   _____

Pronunciation

-s and -es endings

5 🎧 **6.1 Listen and say these words, phrases and sentences.**

1 use
uses
uses a computer
She uses a computer.

2 read
reads
reads the newspaper
He reads the newspaper.

3 listen
listens
listens to music
My friend listens to music.

4 cook
cooks
cooks dinner
My father cooks dinner.

Listen and read

Famous couples

6a 🎧 **6.2 Listen to and/or read the texts about two famous couples.**

b Write answers to the questions about Will Smith and Jada Pinkett Smith.

1 Does Will Smith appear in the film *Men in Black*?
Yes, he does.

2 Where is he from?
_____

3 What is his wife's name?
_____

4 What are their children's names?
_____

5 Where do Will and Jada live now?
_____

c 🎧 **6.3 Listen and check.**

Famous couples

Will Smith and Jada Pinkett Smith

Will Smith is an American actor and rap singer from Philadelphia, USA. He is in the TV series *Fresh Prince of Bel Air* and in the films *Men in Black* (1996) and *Independence Day* (1997). His wife is actress Jada Pinkett Smith. She is in *The Nutty Professor* with Eddie Murphy and in the film *Scream 2*. They have two children – Jaden and Willow – and they live in Los Angeles.

Iman and David Bowie

Iman – her full name is Iman Abdulmajid – is 47 years old and she comes from Somalia in Africa. She is a supermodel, an actress and an international businesswoman. She is married to British rock star and actor David Bowie (real name: David Robert Jones). They both have one child from other marriages and they have a daughter, Alexandra Zahra Jones. They live in New York.

d Write questions for the answers about Iman and David Bowie.

1 _How old is Iman?_
She's 47 years old.

2 _____
She's from Somalia.

3 _____
Yes, she is – to David Bowie.

4 _____
Yes, they have one daughter.

5 _____
They live in New York.

e 🎧 **6.4 Listen and check.**

Grammar focus 2
Present simple questions (*he, she, it*)

7a Look at the picture of Tina and Tony and read their answers to the questions.

	Tina	Tony
Food and drink Do you ... eat meat? drink a lot of coffee?	 No, I'm a vegetarian. No.	 Yes. I love burgers! Yes.
Music Do you ... like rock music? like dancing?	 No, I hate it! Yes.	 Yes. No.
Languages Do you ... study a foreign language? speak French?	 Yes. Yes.	 No ... I only speak English. No.
Free time Do you ... play a sport? like computer games?	 Yes, I play tennis. No.	 No. Yes, I love them!!

b Write questions and answers about Tina and Tony with the words in brackets.

1 (eat meat)

Does Tina eat meat? No, she doesn't.
Does Tony eat meat? Yes, he does.

2 (drink a lot of coffee)

_____
_____

3 (like rock music)

_____
_____

4 (like dancing)

_____
_____

5 (study a foreign language)

_____
_____

6 (speak French)

_____
_____

7 (play a sport)

_____
_____

8 (like computer games)

_____
_____

b 🎧 **6.5 Listen and check.**

Pronunciation
Linking *does he* and *does she*

8 🎧 **6.6 Listen and say these words, phrases and sentences.**

1 Does he ... ?
Does he listen ... ?
Does he listen to music?

2 Does she ... ?
Does she play ... ?
Does she play tennis?

Vocabulary
Likes and dislikes

9a Write what Maria says with the phrases in the box.

....
I don't like   I don't mind   I hate   ~~I like~~   I love
....

Chinese food ☺
1 *'I like Chinese food.'* _____

Robbie Williams ☺
2 ' _____ '

cooking ☹
3 _____

classical music ☺
4 _____

football ☹
5 _____

b 🎧 **6.7 Listen and check.**

Writing
and/but

10a Read the text about Marc and complete the table.

Marc is 26 and is a waiter. He likes cats, but he doesn't like dogs. He likes classical music, but he doesn't like pop music. He plays tennis and listens to live music at the weekend.

Name:	*Marc*
Age:	
Job:	
Likes:	
Doesn't like:	
Weekend activities:	

b Look at the information about Sophie. Write some sentences about her. Use *and* and *but*.

ne: Sophie

: 32

accountant

s: food, reading magazines

sn't like: cooking, reading books

kend activities: computer games, out with friends

Language Live
Making offers

11 Put the words in the correct order.

1 like / Would / coffee / you?
Would you like coffee?

2 some / about / How / popcorn?
_____

3 like / to / something / Would / drink? / you
_____

4 of / please. / water, / A / bottle
_____

12a 🎧 **6.8** Listen and circle what is being offered.

1	chocolate	(sandwich)	popcorn	☐
2	tea	water	coffee	☐
3	a drink	sandwich	tea	☐
4	chocolate	sandwich	popcorn	☐
5	coffee	water	tea	☐

b 🎧 **6.6** Listen again. Does the person say yes (✓) or no (✗)?

13a Put the conversation in the correct order.

1 No thanks. I'm OK. _____
2 Well, yes, please. I love chocolates. _____
3 Would you like a coffee? ___1___
4 How about something to eat? _____
5 Yes, black coffee, please. _____
6 Here you are. _____
7 Are you sure? How about a chocolate? _____

b 🎧 **6.9** Listen and check.

Vocabulary
Daily routines and times

1a Complete the text using the words from the box.

finish	get	~~get up~~	go
have	sleep	start	

My name's Margaret Beech.
I'm a journalist.
I ¹ _get up_ early, at quarter to six, and ² _____ to work at about half past six. I ³ _____ breakfast in a café near my office and ⁴ _____ work at half past seven. I don't ⁵ _____ a big lunch, just a sandwich and a coffee. I usually ⁶ _____ work at about six o'clock. I ⁷ _____ home at seven, then I ⁸ _____ dinner with my husband – he loves cooking! After dinner we usually watch TV, then I ⁹ _____ to bed early, at about ten o'clock and ¹⁰ _____ for seven or eight hours.

b 🎧 **7.1 Listen and check.**

2 Write the times.

1 _eleven o'clock_ **2** _____ **3** _____

4 _____ **5** _____ **6** _____

7 _____ **8** _____

3 Read Lucy's email to her sister and answer the questions.

Hello Mary,

I am a very happy student! I get up at 7.30 a.m. every day and go to university by bus. I don't have breakfast at home; I eat a sandwich on the bus. I have lunch at 1.00 p.m. I always go to a local Italian café and I usually eat pasta. At 4.00 p.m. I finish my lessons and I sometimes go for a walk in the park near the university.

In the evening, I have dinner at 7.00 p.m. at home. I usually study in the evening, but I sometimes go out with friends. How are you?

Love, Lucy

1 When does Lucy get up? .... _at 7.30 a.m._
2 Where does she have breakfast? ....
3 What does she eat for breakfast? ....
4 Where does she eat lunch? ....
5 What does she do at 4.00 p.m.? ....
6 What does she do at 7.00 p.m.? ....
7 When does she study? ....

Grammar focus 1
Frequency adverbs

4a Complete these adverbs of frequency.

1 u s u a l l y
2 a _ _ a _ s
3 n _ _ _ r
4 d _ n ' t u _ _ a _ l _
5 s _ m _ t _ _ e _

b Put the words from exercise 4a in the correct place on the line.

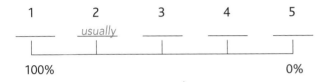

1	2	3	4	5
	usually			

100%   0%

5a Put the adverbs of frequency in the correct place in the sentences below.

> *sometimes*
1 I ∧ get up early. (sometimes)
2 I don't play tennis at the weekend. (usually)
3 My brother and I play football at the weekend. (always)
4 Shops in our town open at night. (sometimes)
5 Barbara doesn't work on Mondays. (usually)
6 I listen to music when I get home. (usually)
7 Children in Britain go to school on Sundays. (never)
8 We go to work by train. (always)

b 🎧 7.2 Listen and check.

Vocabulary
Days of the week

6 Unscramble the days of the week. Number them in the correct order.

1 on Myad   *Monday*   *1*
2 yidarF   _____ _
3 sudyTea   _____ _
4 yanuSd   _____ _
5 adneWeyds   _____ _
6 TuyaSadr   _____ _
7 uysrTadh   _____ _

Listen and read
Life in Britain today

7a 🎧 7.3 Listen to and/or read the text about life in Britain today.

Life in Britain Today

Food
British people like good food and more than half of them go to a restaurant every month. Fast food is also very popular – 30% of all adults have a burger every three months, but 46% have fish and chips!

Sport
British people don't do a lot of sport. Only 17% of people go swimming every week, 9% go cycling and 8% play golf. Football is the most popular sport in Britain; 10% of the population play it and 46% watch it.

Cinema and TV
Films are very popular in Britain and about 60% of people between 15 and 24 go to the cinema every month. At home, men watch TV for about 28 hours every week – two hours more than women.

Holidays
British people love going on holiday and have 56 million holidays a year. The most popular holiday destinations in the UK are Cornwall, Devon, Somerset, Dorset and the South Coast.
British people also like to go abroad on holiday; 27% go to Spain, 10% go to the USA and 9% go to France. Maybe this is because the weather in Britain isn't always very good!

b Listen to and/or read the text again and <u>underline</u> the correct answers in the sentences below.

1 The favourite food in Britain is:
   a) *burgers*   b) *fish and chips*.
2 17% of British people
   a) *go swimming*   b) *play golf*
   c) *play football* **every week**.
3 British men watch about
   a) *28 hours*   b) *30 hours*   c) *2 hours of TV* **a week**.
4 Their favourite holiday destination outside the UK is
   a) *Spain*   b) *France*   c) *the USA*.

Pronunciation
Days of the week

8 🎧 **7.4 Listen and circle the correct pronunciation.**

1	a	ⓑ	**5**	a	b
2	a	b	**6**	a	b
3	a	b	**7**	a	b
4	a	b			

Grammar focus 2
Present simple *Wh-* questions

9a Complete the interview with Chad Martin, a famous Hollywood actor. Use the words in the box.

··
How many   ~~What~~   When   Where
Who   Why
··

1 ___What___ 's the name of your new film?
2 _____ s it in cinemas?
3 _____ do people like your films?
4 _____ 's your favourite actor?
5 _____ 's your wife from?
6 _____ houses do you have?

b Match the questions with the answers.

a Three, I think – no, four! _____
b I love Robert de Niro – he's great! _____
c It's called *Blood in the Afternoon*. ___1___
d She's from Palermo, in Italy. _____
e On Friday. _____
f Because they're fast and exciting, I think. _____

c 🎧 **7.5 Listen and check.**

10a Write questions for the <u>underlined</u> words. Start each question with a question word from exercise 9.

1 <u>About 56 million people</u> live in the UK.
    How many people live in the UK?
2 My brother lives <u>in Egypt</u>.
    _____
3 <u>Bogotá</u> is the capital of Colombia.
    _____
4 <u>Elton John's</u> my favourite singer.
    _____
5 I study English <u>because I want to get a good job.</u>
    _____
6 We usually go to the cinema <u>on Tuesdays</u>.
    _____
7 Monica speaks <u>four</u> languages.
    _____

b 🎧 **7.6 Listen and check.**

Pronunciation
Wh- questions

11 🎧 **7.7 Listen and say these questions.**

1 Who's your favourite actress?
2 Where do you work?
3 When do you go to bed?
4 Why do you study English?
5 What do you do in the evening?
6 How many people are there?

Vocabulary
Prepositions with time expressions

12 Complete the sentences with *on, at, in* or *every*.

1 I don't go to work __on__ Saturdays.
2 I go to the gym ___ day.
3 My father always plays tennis ___ Wednesdays ___ six o'clock.
4 The concert is ___ eight o'clock ___ Monday evening.
5 I drink lots of coffee ___ the morning.
6 I get home ___ seven o'clock ___ the evening.
7 I usually get up ___ six o'clock.
8 I go to the cinema ___ weekend.

Language live
Making an arrangement

13 Put the words in the correct order.

1 you / there. / See
See you there.

2 about / film? / a / How
_____

3 Hall. / There's / at / concert / City / a / the
_____

4 this / you / Are / weekend? / free
_____

5 at / on / o'clock / Friday. / It's / seven
_____

14 Choose the best response to each question.

1 Are you free this Saturday?
a Yes, I think so.
b OK. See you there.
c It starts at 9.00.

2 What time?
a Yes, good idea.
b It's at the *Open House*.
c It starts at 7.30.

3 How about a night out?
a OK. See you there.
b Yes, good idea.
c Yes, I think so.

4 When is the concert?
a It's at the museum.
b It starts at 7.00.
c There's a film at the cinema.

Writing
Making arrangements by text message and email

15 Complete the text messages with the words in the box.

about	cinema	~~free~~	like	Meet
Saturday	See	Why		

Hi, Soren. Are you ¹ *free* on ² ___ ?

Hi, Birta. I think so. ³ ___ ?

How ⁴ ___ a film? *Thor* is on at the Odeon ⁵ ___ at 7.15. Good. I'd ⁶ ___ to see that.

⁷ ___ me at the cinema at 7? Great. ⁸ ___ you there.

16a Read Lee's email to Anna.

> Hi Anna, I'm home for the weekend! Are you free on Saturday evening? How about a night out?
> Where can we meet? When?
> Lee x

b Put the sentences in Anna's email to Lee in the correct order.

a Are you free on Sunday? ___
b I'm sorry but I can't go out with you on Saturday. ___
c Hi Lee, ___
d Anna x ___
e It's my Dad's birthday. ___
f Thanks for your email. ___

c Write Lee's email reply to Anna. Include these things:

- a greeting
- say you are free on Sunday
- suggest a place and time
- a message ending

_____
_____
_____
_____
_____
_____
_____
_____

Vocabulary
Verbs – things you do

1 Match the verbs from the box with the pictures.

play ride run swim walk

1 _play_   the guitar

2 _____

3 _____ a bicycle

4 _____

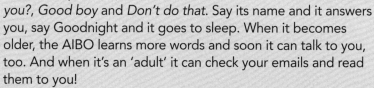

5 _____

Listen and read
AIBO – the electronic pet

2a 🎧 **8.1** Listen to and/or read the text. Tick (✓) the things an AIBO does, according to the text.

talk	☐	run	☐
dance	☐	play chess	☐
ride a bicycle	☐	swim	☐
play the guitar	☐	play ball	☐
sing	☐	take photographs	☐
walk	☐	check emails	☐

AIBO – the electronic pet

What exactly is an AIBO, and why do people love them so much?

An AIBO is a robot dog, about 28 centimetres long and it can do lots of amazing things. For example, it can walk, run, play with a ball, be happy or sad – just like a real dog! It can also dance, sing songs, see colours and take photographs like a camera!

A new (or 'baby') AIBO can't see or hear, but it can understand about 40 words and phrases like *How old are you?*, *Good boy* and *Don't do that*. Say its name and it answers you, say Goodnight and it goes to sleep. When it becomes older, the AIBO learns more words and soon it can talk to you, too. And when it's an 'adult' it can check your emails and read them to you!

These robot pets are very popular in Japan and the USA, but they aren't cheap. Each AIBO is about $7,500 – so maybe a real dog is better!

b Listen to and/or read the text again. Are these sentences true (T) or false (F)?

1 It's very big.   _F_
2 It takes photographs.   _____
3 Baby AIBOs see and hear very well.   _____
4 It understands things people say to it. _____
5 It checks your email.   _____
6 Adult AIBOs talk.   _____
7 It's very expensive.   _____

Grammar focus 1
can/can't

3a Complete the sentences with *can* or *can't*.

1 I *can* ride a bicycle, but I *can't* swim.
2 Margie's always late for work because she _____ get up early.

3 Their daughter's only six months old, so she _____ talk or read.
4 I'm sorry, I _____ understand this sentence.
5 I _____ play chess, but I don't often win!
6 My husband _____ cook very well. The food he makes is delicious!
7 Joe _____ speak French and Spanish fluently, but he _____ speak Chinese.
8 My sister _____ play the violin brilliantly.

b 🎧 **8.2** Listen and check.

Pronunciation
can/can't

4 🎧 **8.3** Listen to the sentences. Circle the word you hear.

1 (can)	can't		**6** can	can't
2 can	can't		**7** can	can't
3 can	can't		**8** can	can't
4 can	can't		**9** can	can't
5 can	can't		**10** can	can't

Grammar focus 2
Questions with *can*

5a Write questions using *can* and the prompts.

1 you / dance?   *Can you dance?*
2 he / swim?   _____
3 they / play the guitar? _____
4 she / ride a bike?   _____
5 she / swim?   _____
6 you / drive a car?   _____
7 he / run fast?   _____
8 they / cook?   _____

b 🎧 **8.4** Listen and check.

6a Complete the answers.

1 Can you cook?
  Yes, *I can* _____ .
2 Can your parents speak English?
  No, _____ .
3 Can Jim play football well?
  No, _____ .
4 Can your daughter read and write?
  Yes, _____ .
5 Can you swim?
  No, _____ .
6 Can your son read music?
  Yes, _____ .
7 Can your friends play tennis?
  Yes, _____ .

b 🎧 **8.5** Listen and check. Practise saying the questions and short answers.

Vocabulary
Parts of the body

7 Write the parts of the body.

1 *head*

2 _____

3 _____

4 _____

5 _____

6 _____

7 _____

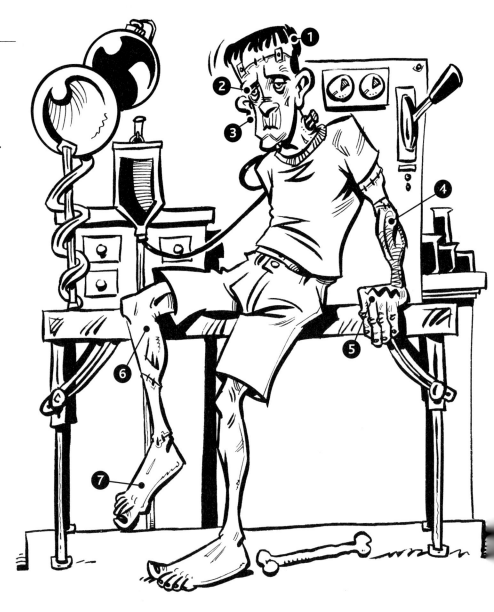

Grammar focus 3
Review of questions

8 Put the words in the correct order to make questions.

1 Ali / a / drive / Can / car?
   Can Ali drive a car?

2 gym / day? / you / go / every / Do / to / the
   _____

3 does / for / What / breakfast? / eat / Maria
   _____

4 play / When / they / tennis? / do
   _____

5 you / swim / Can / kilometre? / a
   _____

6 can / How / run? / you / kilometres /many
   _____

7 good / numbers? / at / Is / remembering / she / phone
   _____

8 to / Do / going / galleries? / like / art / you
   _____

9 basketball? / they / Where / play / do / usually
   _____

10 musical / you / a / instrument? / play / Can
   _____

9 Match the questions with the answers.

1 Can you run five kilometres? ☐ e
2 What is Andy interested in? ☐
3 When does Sheila go to the gym? ☐
4 Do you go out with friends every weekend? ☐
5 Are you interested in cooking? ☐
6 Can Lauren touch her toes? ☐

a Sport.
b Yes, she can.
c Every Tuesday.
d No, I'm not, but I love eating!
e No, I can't.
f Yes, I do.

Writing
Describing your skills and interests

10   Read the text about Zafar. Put capital letters in the correct places.

M
~~my~~ name's zafar and i'm 23 years old. i'm from islamabad in pakistan. i'm not good at languages, but i can speak urdu and punjabi. i can't speak english very well, but i want to study business at university in england. i'm interested in music, but i can't play a musical instrument. i'm a very sporty person and i can play football well.

11   Complete Jenny's paragraph about her skills and interests using the information below.

Name: Jenny
Age: 24
From: Nha Trang, Vietnam
Good at languages: ✓
Languages: Vietnamese, English, French, a little Chinese
Interested in: taking photographs
Wants to study: Art and photography
Not interested in: music
Plays musical instrument: ✗
Likes: dancing at the weekend
Sports/games: not sporty but can swim well

Hi, my name's Jenny and I'm ...

Language live
Making requests

12a Complete the dialogue with the words in the box.

can	can't	course	don't
~~Excuse~~	me	please	tell
Yes	you		

Woman: [1]_Excuse_ me, [2]_____ you tell me the time, please?

Man: Yes, of [3]_____ . It's 12 o'clock.

Woman: Thanks. Can you [4]_____ me where the Eiffel Tower is?

Man: [5]_____ , it's on the left bank.

Woman: The left bank? Can I look at your map, [6]_____ ?

Man: Sorry, I [7]_____ have one.

Woman: Oh, well can [8]_____ take [9]_____ to the Eiffel Tower, please?

Man: No, I [10]_____ . I'm sorry, but I'm late!

b 🎧 8.6 Listen and check.

35

Vocabulary
Months of the year

1 Write the months and put them in the correct order.

1 Y A M

_____ ___

2 R E S T B P E M E

_____ ___

3 Y A N R U J A

_January_____ _1_ _1_

4 G U T A S U

_____ ___

5 M E E N B R O V

_____ ___

6 C R O O T E B

_____ ___

7 C H A R M

_____ ___

8 B E E R C E D M

_____ ___

9 U Y L J

_____ ___

10 B Y E R R A U F

_____ ___

11 P L A I R

_____ ___

12 E N U J

_____ ___

Pronunciation
Months of the year

2 🎧 9.1 Listen and circle the correct stress pattern for each month.

1	January	●•••	•●••	••●•
2	February	●•••	●•••	••●•
3	April	●•	•●	
4	July	●•	•●	
5	August	●•	•●	
6	September	●••	•●•	••●
7	October	●••	•●•	•●•
8	November	●••	•●•	•●●
9	December	●••	•●•	••●

Vocabulary
Ordinal numbers and dates

3 Write the ordinal numbers.

1	sixth	_6th_
2	twelfth	___
3	first	___
4	fifth	___
5	second	___
6	tenth	___
7	seventeenth	___
8	twentieth	___
9	third	___
10	fourth	___
11	eleventh	___
12	twenty-first	___

4 🎧 9.2 Listen and complete the dates.

1 _14th_ February
2 28th _____
3 2nd _____
4 ___ June
5 ___ November
6 ___ August
7 8th _____
8 15th _____
9 ___ July
10 ___ _____
11 ___ _____
12 ___ _____

Listen and read
When they were young

5a Match the names in the box with the photos of the people below.

Arnold Schwarzenegger   Barrack Obama   Ricky Martin

b Match these sentences with the people. There are four sentences for each person.

1 He was born in Puerto Rico, in the Caribbean, in 1971.	*Ricky Martin*
2 He was born in 1947 in a small village near Graz, in Austria.	_____
3 He was born in Honolulu, Hawaii, in 1961.	_____

4 His family was very poor and life in Austria was difficult.	_____
5 From the age of 12 to 17 he was a singer in the Latin-American pop band *Menudo*.	_____
6 At school he was called 'O'Bomber' because he was good at basketball.	_____

7 His first job was in an ice cream shop and now he doesn't like ice cream.	_____
8 His song, *La Copa de la Vida*, was the official 1998 Football World Cup song.	_____
9 He was very good at sports, especially bodybuilding, and in 1972 he was 'Mr Universe'.	_____

10 He's now a famous actor and politician, and lives in the United States.	_____
11 Now he's a politician and he became the President of the United States in 2009.	_____
12 He's now a famous singer and he can speak five languages fluently!	_____

c 🎧 **9.3** Listen and check.

Grammar focus 1
Past simple of *be*: *was/were*

6 Complete the sentences about 1980 with *was* or *were*.

In 1980
1 Margaret Thatcher __was__ Prime Minister of Britain.
2 there _____ 4.4 billion people in the world.
3 the Olympic Games _____ in Moscow.
4 Bjorn Borg _____ a very famous tennis player.

5 Tom Cruise _____ only eighteen years old.
6 East Germany and West Germany _____ different countries.
7 *The Elephant Man* and *Friday the 13th* _____ popular films.
8 Jimmy Carter _____ the President of the United States.

7a Rewrite these sentences as negatives.

1 He was very rich.
   He wasn't very rich.
2 They were from Japan.
   _____
3 There was a supermarket in the square.
   _____
4 Their car was very expensive.
   _____
5 Marco's grandmother was French.
   _____
6 His parents were poor.
   _____
7 My brothers were at home last night.
   _____

b 🎧 9.4 Listen and check.

8a <u>Underline</u> the correct word to complete the text.

'My name's Niall Kelly, and I ¹**was** / **were** born in 1946, in a village called Mallahyde, in Ireland. My father, Donald, ²**was** / **were** an engineer, and Maeve, my mother, ³**was** / **were** a nurse. There ⁴**was** / **were** six people in our family: my parents, my three sisters and me. My sisters ⁵**was** / **were** usually very noisy, but I ⁶**was** / **were** a quiet child. I ⁷**wasn't** / **weren't** happy at my first school. I ⁸**wasn't** / **weren't** good at maths or English, but I⁹**was** / **were** good at sport, especially football. I remember my best friends ¹⁰**was** / **were** two brothers called Jim and Adam, and they ¹¹**wasn't** / **weren't** good at school, they ¹²**was** / **were** always very naughty in class! I also remember my favourite food – it ¹³**was** / **were** hot bread!'

b 🎧 9.5 Listen and check.

Grammar focus 2
Questions with *was/were*

9a Put the words in the correct order to make questions.

1 job? / was / What / his
  What was his job?

2 were / Where / from? / they
  _____

3 for class? / were / late / Why / you
  _____

4 last night? / What / on TV / was
  _____

5 you / were / Who / yesterday afternoon? / with
  _____

6 at school / Was / yesterday? / Michel
  _____

7 was / grandmother's name? / your / What
  _____

8 both your parents / Were / Russia? / from
  _____

b 🎧 **9.6 Listen and check. Practise saying the questions.**

10 Read Niall's story in Exercise 8 again. Write short answers to these questions.

1 Was Niall born in Ireland?   *Yes, he was.*
2 Was his father a doctor?   _____
3 Was his mother a nurse?   _____
4 Were his sisters usually noisy?   _____
5 Was he happy at his first school?   _____
6 Was he good at maths?   _____
7 Was he good at sport?   _____
8 Were Jim and Adam naughty in class?   _____

Vocabulary
Years

11a Write these years.

1 1942   *nineteen forty-two*
2 1999   _____
3 2007   _____
4 1856   _____
5 2001   _____
6 1865   _____

b 🎧 **9.7 Listen and check. Practise saying the years.**

Writing
Write about your childhood

12a Write answers to these questions about your childhood.

1 Where and when were you born?
  _____

2 How many people are there in your family?
  _____

3 Were you a happy / unhappy / noisy / quiet / naughty / good child?
  _____

4 Were you happy at your first school?
  _____

5 What were/weren't you good at?
  _____

6 Who was your best friend?
  _____

7 What was your favourite food / book / film / game?
  _____

b Write a paragraph about your childhood.

I was born in . . .

Grammar focus 1
Past simple: regular verbs (positive)

1 Write the Past simple of these regular verbs.

1 start	_started_	**5** talk	_____
2 like	_____	**6** want	_____
3 hate	_____	**7** return	_____
4 listen	_____	**8** marry	_____

2a Complete the sentences using the Past simple tense of the verbs in the box.

> die   ~~live~~   play   start   study
> walk   watch   work

1 My wife __lived__ in Colombia when she was young.
2 Their father _____ when he was 86.
3 My grandfather _____ for a British company.
4 We _____ the Past simple in class today.
5 Dylan _____ computer games all night.
6 Last night, I _____ a really good film on TV.
7 Gabriela _____ her new job two days ago.
8 It was a beautiful day, so I _____ to work.

b 🎧 **10.1 Listen and check.**

Pronunciation
Past simple -*ed* endings

3 🎧 **10.2 Listen and put the words in the box in the correct column.**

> cooked   hated   listened   lived   loved
> moved   painted   played   returned
> walked   wanted   watched

/d/	/t/	/id/
moved	_____	_____
_____	_____	_____
_____	_____	_____
_____		
_____		

Grammar focus 2
Past simple: regular verbs (negative)

4 Read the information about Nick, his wife and his parents. Rewrite the sentences as negatives.

Last year
1 Nick returned to the UK.
Nick didn't return to the UK.
2 he lived in London.
_____
_____
3 he worked in an office.
_____
_____
4 he studied French.
_____
_____

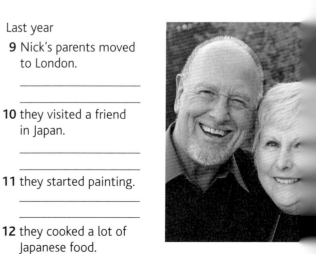

Last year
5 Catherine married Nick.
_____
_____
6 she played guitar at a concert in London.
_____
_____
7 she received a music prize.
_____
_____
8 she listened to a lot of music.
_____
_____

Last year
9 Nick's parents moved to London.
_____
_____
10 they visited a friend in Japan.
_____
_____
11 they started painting.
_____
_____
12 they cooked a lot of Japanese food.
_____
_____

Vocabulary

Verbs – life events

5 Tick (✓) the words that go with the verb, and cross (✗) the words that don't. There is one wrong word for each verb.

1

go to

university	✓
school	✓
your driving test	✗

2

get

university	____
married	____
a job	____

3

buy

a house	____
your first job	____
an apartment	____

4

start

university	____
your partner	____
work	____

5

leave

school	____
university	____
married	____

6

meet

your partner	____
a good friend	____
work	____

7

have

a child	____
a daughter	____
married	____

Listen and read

The Kennedys

6a What do you know about the Kennedy family? Was John F Kennedy famous because he was

  1 a businessman?
  2 a president of the USA?
  3 a footballer?

b 🎧 10.3 Listen to and/or read the story of the Kennedy family to check your answer.

The Kennedys

John F Kennedy is probably the most famous President in American history, but the story of the Kennedy family is not a happy one.

John was born in Boston, USA in 1917. The Kennedys were a big family and John had five sisters and three brothers. His father, Joseph Kennedy, was a businessman and his mother Rose was the daughter of a politician.

After university, John worked as a journalist, then became a politician in 1946. But this was an unhappy time for the Kennedy family – John's brother, Joe died in the Second World War and four years later, his sister, Kathleen died in a plane crash.

John became a Senator* in 1952, the same year he met his wife, Jacqueline Bouvier. They got married in 1953 and had three children – but their third child, Patrick, died two days after he was born.

In 1961, John F Kennedy became President, and he was very popular with the American people. He died in Dallas, Texas in November 1963 and his brother Bobby also died five years later.

The Kennedys are a famous family, but their story is a very sad one.

* a Senator = a member of the American Senate

c Listen to and/or read the text again. Are these sentences true (T) or false (F), according to the text? Correct the false sentences.

> Boston

1 John F Kennedy was born in ~~Washington~~. ___F___
2 Joseph and Rose Kennedy had nine children. ____
3 Two of their children died in the 1940s. ____
4 John got married three years after he became a Senator. ____
5 John and Jacqueline's third child died when he was very young. ____
6 John F Kennedy became President in 1963. ____
7 Bobby Kennedy died in 1968. ____

Grammar focus 3
Past simple: irregular verbs (positive and negative)

7a Write the Past simple of the verbs in the clues in the crossword.

Clues

Across ➜	Down ⬇
1 sell	**2** leave
3 buy	**3** become
5 make	**4** have
7 go	**6** meet

```
          ¹S  O  ²L  D
                   
                   
        ³         ⁴
      ⁵          
                 
            ⁶    
        ⁷        
```

b Complete the sentences using the Past simple of the verbs in exercise 7a.

1 Joanna __left__ home when she was 18.
2 Last night, I _____ to the cinema.
3 They _____ their car to a friend's son for £2,000.
4 Alfred Hitchcock _____ 53 films in his life.
5 My parents _____ this house when they moved here in 1964.
6 She _____ an actress after she left school.
7 When we were children, we _____ a dog.
8 Erica _____ her husband when she was on holiday.

c 🎧 **10.4** Listen and check.

8 Correct the mistakes. There is one mistake in each sentence.

1 My brother ~~were~~ born in 1972.   _was_
2 We have our first child last month.   ___
3 I didn't went to work yesterday.   ___
4 I meet her three years ago.   ___
5 Cecilia started work after she leaved university.   ___
6 Steve didn't sold his house.   ___
7 Charlie Chaplin maked a lot of money.   ___

Vocabulary
Creative jobs

9 Label the photos with the words in the box.

architect   ~~artist~~   dancer   film director
inventor   musician   singer   writer

1 ___artist___

2 _____

3 _____

4 _____

5 _____

6 _____

7 _____

8 _____

Writing
A personal history

10a Look at the information about Alicia Ojeda and complete the text.

name:	Alicia Ojeda
born:	1965, Buenos Aires, Argentina
parents:	mother – housewife father – doctor
brothers / sisters:	one brother, Javier one sister, Carolina
school:	started – 1970 left – 1987
university:	yes – English and French
first job:	teacher
partner:	met Roberto – 1993
married:	yes – 1996
children:	one son, Franco
job now:	architect
lives now:	New York
other information:	writes books; goes swimming

Alicia Ojeda was born in ¹*Buenos Aires* in 1965. Her
father was a doctor and her mother was a ²_____ .
She has one brother, Javier and one ³_____ ,
Carolina. She started school in ⁴_____ and left
school in 1987. She went to university and studied
⁵_____ and French, then she started work as a
⁶_____ . She met her partner, Roberto in
⁷_____ and they got married in 1996. They have
one ⁸_____ , Franco. Now Alicia works as a
⁹_____ . and lives in New York. She also writes
books, and in her free time she goes ¹⁰_____ .

b Write a personal history about someone you know.

Language live
Apologies and thanks

11a Complete the texts and emails with the words in the box.

> delay   fantastic   questions   Sorry
> ~~Thanks~~   tomorrow

1

Thanks for the card. I was in hospital for a week
and am happy to be home now. Please visit. Jim

2

Thanks for the chocolates.
They are _____. Love, Dad x

3

Thanks for the invitation. I can come! See you
_____ at seven o'clock. _____ I didn't
answer yesterday – I was in a meeting all day.

4

Sorry for the _____. Here is the information
for your presentation on Monday. Hope this
is OK. Please phone or email if you have any
_____. Regards, Jo.

b Match the texts and emails in exercise 11a with the following answers.

a That's OK. I'm really pleased you can come.
See you tomorrow.   _3_
b You're welcome. Happy birthday!   ___
c Thanks for this. Can we meet and have a
coffee before the presentation?   ___
d Good to hear that you're home. I can come
to see you on Thursday at 2 p.m. OK?   ___

12 🎧 10.5 Listen to the phrases. Write A (apology),
T (thanks) or R (response).

1 _A_   6 ___
2 ___   7 ___
3 ___   8 ___
4 ___   9 ___
5 ___   10 ___

13 Write an appropriate response to these phrases.

1 I'm sorry.   _____
2 Thank you.   _____
3 That's very kind.   _____
4 I'm sorry I'm late.   _____
5 I bought you some flowers.
  Happy birthday!   _____

Vocabulary
Transport and travel

1 Unscramble the transport words.

1 ARC	*car*	**5** SHPI	_____
2 RITAN	_____	**6** SUB	_____
3 EKBI	_____	**7** ENPLA	_____
4 XTAI	_____	**8** TBAO	_____

Listen and read
The only way to travel

2a 🎧 **11.1** Listen to and/or read the text. Choose the correct answer.

The first Orient Express travelled:
1 from London to Paris.
2 from London to Istanbul.
3 from Paris to Istanbul.
4 from Paris to Bulgaria.
5 from Strasbourg to Istanbul.

The only way to travel

In 1865, a Belgian man, Georges Nagelmackers, had an idea. He wanted to build a train to travel across Europe and into Asia. Nagelmackers saw Pullman's sleeper cars on the trains in America. Passengers slept on the journey and it was comfortable. Nagelmackers decided to design a train with sleeper cars for Europe. He wanted his train to be fantastic – like a really good hotel inside.

On 4th October, 1883, his train departed from the train station the *Gare de Strasbourg* in Paris. It was called *The Orient Express.* Everybody wanted to travel on *The Orient Express.* Famous passengers were King Ferdinand of Bulgaria, King Leopold the 3rd of Belgium and Czar Nicholas the 2nd of Russia. There were also lots of journalists on the train.

The journey went from Paris in France to Istanbul in Turkey, and it took four days. The first passengers enjoyed the journey so much that everyone wanted to travel on *The Orient Express.*

You can travel on *The Orient Express* today, but it isn't the original one.

b Choose the correct alternative to complete the sentences.

1 *The Orient Express* is a **train** / **boat**.
2 **Nagelmackers** / **Pullman** designed *The Orient Express*.
3 Nagelmackers was from **America** / **Belgium**.
4 The first journey was in **1865** / **1883**.
5 The train was **fantastic** / **awful** inside.
6 There **were** / **weren't** any journalists on the first journey.
7 The journey took **three** / **four** days.
8 The train **was** / **wasn't** popular.
9 You **can** / **can't** travel on the original *Orient Express* today.

Grammar focus 1
Past simple: *Yes/No* questions

3 Look at the picture and put the words in the correct order to make questions.

1 to the beach / Stephanie / Did / go
Did Stephanie go to the beach _____?

2 Did / go / swimming / Bob
_____?

3 happy / Were / the children
_____?

4 the hotel / like / Bob / Did
_____?

5 nice / Was / the beach
_____?

6 the hotel / Carla and Matthew / Did / like
_____?

7 Carla and Matthew / go / Did / shopping
_____?

8 happy / Bob / Was
_____?

b 🎧 **11.2** Listen and check.

4 Look at the information in the table. Write short answers for the questions in exercise 3a.

	Stephanie	Bob	Carla and Matthew
like the hotel	yes	no	yes
go to the beach	yes	yes	yes
go swimming	no	no	yes
like the beach	yes	yes	yes
go shopping	yes	yes	no
have a good time	yes	no	yes

1 *Yes, she did.*
2 _____
3 _____
4 _____
5 _____
6 _____
7 _____
8 _____

Pronunciation
Linking words

6 🎧 **11.4** Listen and repeat.
1 Were you?
2 Were you happy?
3 Were you tired after work?
4 Were you late?
5 Were you on time?
6 Did you?
7 Did you go?
8 Did you buy a return ticket?
9 Did you have a good journey?
10 Did you go on a train journey?

Grammar focus 2
Past simple: *Wh-* questions

5a Complete the questions about these famous people.

Indira Gandhi was born in India in 1917 and went to university in England. She got married in 1942 and became Prime Minister of India in 1966. She had two children and died in 1984.

Jimi Hendrix was born in the USA in 1942 and started playing the guitar when he was sixteen.
He went to London in 1966 and made his first record, *Hey Joe*, in 1967. He made four albums before he died on September 18th, 1970.

Fyodor Dostoevsky was born in Moscow in 1821 and he had six brothers and sisters. He lived in St Petersburg and died in 1881 at the age of sixty. He wrote eight books, including *Crime and Punishment* and *The Brothers Karamazov*.

1 *Where did* she *go* to university?
   In England.
2 When _____ she _____ married?
   In 1942.
3 _____ _____ she _____ Prime Minister?
   In 1966.
4 How _____ children _____ _____ _____ ?
   Two.

5 _____ _____ he _____ playing the guitar?
   When he was sixteen.
6 Where _____ _____ _____ in 1966?
   He went to London.
7 _____ _____ albums _____ _____ make?
   Four.
8 _____ _____ _____ die?
   On the 18th of September, 1970.

9 How _____ brothers and sisters _____ he _____ ?
   Six.
10 Where _____ _____ _____ ?
   In St Petersburg.
11 _____ _____ he _____ ?
   In 1881.
12 How _____ books _____ _____ _____ ?
   Eight.

b 🎧 **11.3** Listen and check. Practise saying the questions.

7 Circle the correct alternative to complete the questions.

1 When **did** / **(was)** / **were** he born?
2 What **did** / **was** / **were** you do last night?
3 Where **did** / **was** / **were** you at nine o'clock this morning?
4 Why **did** / **was** / **were** she get up early?
5 How much money **was** / **did** / **were** you take on holiday?
6 Who **were** / **was** / **did** you go with?
7 How long **were** / **was** / **did** you there for?

Vocabulary
Time phrases

8 Put these expressions in order.

yesterday afternoon	_____
ten minutes ago	__1__
fifty years ago	_____
last night	_____
in 1997	_____
three months ago	_____
two hours ago	__2__
last week	_____
last month	_____
yesterday morning	_____

9 Complete the text with the words in the box.

First	for twelve hours	In the end	then
~~twelve years ago~~	2010		

I hate boats, I can't swim and I get seasick. I first went on a boat ¹*twelve years ago*. It was awful, I was very sick. I didn't want to ever go on a boat again, but in ²_____ my best friend decided to get married and the wedding was - on a boat! The boat travelled from Seattle in the USA to Vancouver in Canada. ³_____ , we took the train to Seattle, ⁴_____ , we got on the boat and sailed to Vancouver. The wedding lasted ⁵_____ . I wasn't seasick, but I wasn't very happy. ⁶_____ , we got to Vancouver and I stayed in a lovely hotel for the weekend – that was fantastic!

Holiday activities

10 Put the words in the box with the correct verb.

a boat trip	a restaurant	shopping	sightseeing
skiing	museums	~~out~~	walking

Eat	_out_			
Go	_____	_____	_____	_____
Go on	_____			
Go to	_____			
Visit	_____			

Writing
A blog about a journey

11 Judith and Greg are American. They are on holiday in Europe. Read their blog and tick the things they talk about.

How old they are	☐
Where they live	☐
Where they are	☐
Where they travelled from	☐
When they arrived	☐
How they travelled	☐
How they feel	☐
The weather	☐
The food	☐
Their children	☐

We're here in Madrid and very excited! We arrived at 10 p.m. The flight from New York was fine but long (about eight hours on the plane). We didn't watch any movies during the flight. We had a big dinner and lots of tea. We slept well.

Madrid is fantastic. It's hot – about 30°C – and we are happy to be here.

We're at the hotel now. We had a hot shower and a good breakfast. We want to go out now.

Tomorrow – Paris!

12 Write Judith and Greg's blog from Paris. Use the blog from Madrid and the pictures below to help you.

1 Atocha station in Madrid 18.30 Tuesday

5 Beds not so good ☹

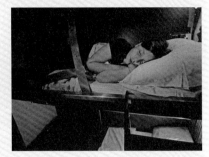

2 Hurray! We're in Paris 9.30 a.m. Wednesday

6 Beds here are excellent ☺

3 Our train

7 The Louvre after lunch today

4 Dinner was fantastic!

8 The weather in Paris

_____
_____
_____
_____
_____
_____

Language live

Travelling by train

13 🎧 **11.5** Listen to a conversation at a train station. Put the conversation in the correct order.

Single or return?	___
What time is the next train?	___
That's £33.50.	___
Platform 4.	___
Yes, please?	_1_
Thank you.	___
It's at 16.12.	___
Which platform?	___
Can I have a ticket to York, please?	___
You're welcome.	___
Return, please.	___

14 🎧 **11.6** Listen to another conversation at a train station. Are these sentences true (T) or false (F)?

1 The man wants to go to Liverpool. _T_
2 He buys a return ticket. ___
3 The ticket costs £52.16. ___
4 The next train is at 10.30. ___
5 The train leaves from Platform 3. ___

12 WHAT DO YOU WANT?

Vocabulary
Verb phrases about wants

1 Match the words and phrases in A with the words and phrases in B to make verb phrases.

A	B
1 go	**a** singing group
2 perform	**b** round the world
3 travel	**c** a cat
4 do a course	**d** diving
5 join a	**e** a football team
6 get	**f** on stage
7 start	**g** in jewellery making

Grammar focus 1
want and want to

2a Put these words in the correct order.

1 tonight. / I / to watch TV / want
I want to watch TV tonight.

2 you / want / shopping? / go / to / Do
_____

3 don't. / I / No,
_____

4 a film / I / to see / this afternoon. / want
_____

5 to go out / want / I / don't / tomorrow.
_____

6 after the lesson. / I / a cup of coffee / want
_____

7 my homework / tonight. / I / to do / want / don't
_____

8 he / want / come to the café? / to / Does
_____

9 does / he / Yes,
_____

10 do you / tomorrow? / What / want / to do
_____

b 🎧 12.1 Listen and check. Practise saying the sentences.

Pronunciation
Linking with want

3a 🎧 12.2 Listen and circle which phrase you hear.

1	want a	(want to)
2	want a	want to
3	want a	want to
4	want a	want to
5	want a	want to
6	want a	want to

b Listen again. Practise saying the sentences aloud.

Vocabulary
Things you can buy

4a Unscramble the words to find eight things you can buy.

1 kejtac	_____	**5** neaigsrr	_____
2 laburelm	_____	**6** letwal	_____
3 sjane	_____	**7** rfsac	_____
4 sirht t	_____	**8** hatwc	_____

b Find the words from exercise 4a in the word square.

w	a	l	e	j	a	c	k	e	t	s	a
h	d	f	e	e	j	w	s	c	j	i	l
e	q	t	s	a	w	d	o	p	r	t	e
a	f	r	a	n	l	s	r	l	g	s	e
r	w	a	t	s	o	c	o	e	w	h	l
r	u	k	e	r	w	a	t	c	h	i	v
i	d	k	m	s	y	r	i	n	b	r	e
n	a	m	a	r	d	f	g	k	e	t	i
g	x	b	n	e	a	w	u	p	s	c	a
s	u	m	b	r	e	l	l	a	t	r	e
e	h	f	j	u	m	b	r	a	a	l	l
t	s	h	e	v	w	a	l	l	e	t	i

Grammar focus 2
going to

5 Put *am*, *are* or *is* in the gaps below. Use contractions (*'m*, *'re*, *'s*) where possible.

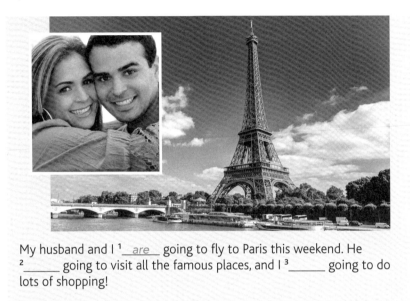

My husband and I ¹ _are_ going to fly to Paris this weekend. He ² _____ going to visit all the famous places, and I ³ _____ going to do lots of shopping!

We ⁴ _____ going to visit my sister there – she lives in Paris. Our children ⁵ _____ going to stay at home with my mother.

It's my birthday tomorrow, and I ⁶ _____ going to see a concert with some friends. Then we ⁷ _____ going to have dinner in a nice restaurant.

My parents ⁸ _____ going to buy me a new laptop for my birthday!

6a Write sentences about the future with the words below.

1 I / play tennis this weekend.
   I'm going to play tennis this weekend.
2 He / not / have lunch with his sister.
   He isn't going to have lunch with his sister.
3 They / see the Taj Mahal next week.
   _____
4 Chris / not / buy a mobile phone.
   _____
5 We / see a film this evening.
   _____
6 I / visit my friend Mark in hospital.
   _____
7 Margie and Vanessa / not / buy any clothes next weekend.
   _____
8 Luca / start a new job on Monday.
   _____

b 🎧 **12.3 Listen and check.**

7a Choose the correct answer.

1 **a** Are he going to
   b Is you going to   phone
   c Are you going to   Jack?

2 **a** What are you going
   b What are you   do
      going to   tonight?
   c What you are going to

3 **a** Where you are going
   b Where are you   go on
      going to   holiday?
   c Where's you going

4 **a** Are your parents going to
   b Is your parents   move
      going to   house?
   c Your parents are going to

5 **a** What's Bob going
   b What's Bob   study at
      going to   university?
   c What Bob going to

6 **a** Is she going to   study
   b Are she going to   English
   c She is going to   next year?

b 🎧 **12.4 Listen and check.**

Pronunciation
going to

8 🎧 **12.5 Listen and repeat.**

1 going to visit
2 Are you going to visit?
3 going to see
4 Are you going to see Jim?
5 going to have
6 I'm going to have breakfast.
7 going to buy
8 They're going to buy a card.
9 going to cook
10 She's going to cook dinner.

49

Vocabulary
Describing objects: colours and sizes

9a Find a colour word in each line.

D	G	G	R	E	E	N	N	G	T	U	Y
B	R	E	D	L	E	J	G	S	E	W	N
S	C	H	E	E	Y	E	L	L	O	W	Y
T	E	N	L	O	R	A	N	G	E	A	T
B	L	U	E	G	E	T	A	B	L	E	S
N	M	D	F	T	B	P	U	R	P	L	E
S	N	B	R	O	W	N	H	B	R	S	J
A	W	H	I	T	E	E	C	R	I	G	O
N	R	L	B	L	A	C	K	I	L	K	W
Y	S	H	G	H	W	A	G	R	E	Y	T

b Unscramble the size words.

1 galer   _large_   **3** axert gelar _____

2 iummde _____   **4** lmals _____

Listen and read
Holiday destinations

10a 🎧 12.6 Where are you going to go on holiday this year? Listen to and/or read these descriptions of three famous holiday destinations.

Holiday destinations

Paris

Paris, the capital of France, is a great place for a holiday. You can visit famous buildings and museums like the Eiffel Tower and the Louvre. Or you can go shopping along the Champs Élysées and have a drink or a meal in one of the many cafés and restaurants. You can travel along the River Seine by boat or go for a walk in the Luxembourg Gardens, one of the many beautiful parks in the city. Paris is also the home of many famous artists. Picasso, Toulouse Lautrec and Rodin all lived in Paris. So, come and stay for a weekend or a month … there's always lots to do in Paris!

Istanbul

The Turkish city of Istanbul is a wonderful place to visit. In the old part of the city there are lots of interesting buildings, like the 500-year-old Topkapi Palace. There are also two beautiful mosques very near the Palace; the Sancta Sophia and the famous Blue Mosque. Most visitors to Istanbul go shopping in the city's biggest market, the 'Grand Bazaar'. There are more than four thousand shops there and you can buy books, food, clothes, flowers and carpets. The food in Istanbul is great and the city has some fantastic fish restaurants. So, come and visit Istanbul – the city where Asia meets Europe!

Hong Kong

You can't visit Hong Kong without shopping! There are many beautiful department stores, boutiques and markets in Hong Kong where you can buy everything from food and clothes to interesting souvenirs. Hong Kong is also great for eating out. There are over 11,000 restaurants in Hong Kong, so you can eat wonderful Chinese food in a different place every day. Hong Kong is a busy place, but there are many parks and other quiet places where you can sit and look at the fantastic views. Come and visit Hong Kong …there's nowhere like it!

b Listen to and/or read the texts again. Are these sentences true (T) or false (F)?

1 Paris is the capital of France. _T_

2 You can go shopping in the Champs Élysées. ___

3 You can travel along the River Seine by train. ___

4 The Blue Mosque is in the old part of Istanbul. ___

5 There are 400 shops in the Grand Bazaar. ___

6 There are some good fish restaurants in Istanbul. ___

7 There are 1,000 restaurants in Hong Kong. ___

8 There aren't any quiet places in Hong Kong. ___

Language live
Saying goodbye

11 Put the words in the correct order.

1 you / See / again.
See you again

2 nice / a / Have / weekend.

3 on / you / See / Monday.

4 miss / going / you. / to / We're

5 job. / Good / your / in / luck / new

12 Choose the best response.

1 Have a nice weekend.
   a Thanks. See you on Monday.
   b Good luck in your new job.
2 This is for you.
   a Thanks, everyone.
   b Thanks for everything.
3 I'm going home. See you tomorrow.
   a See you again.
   b See you tomorrow.
4 Good luck in your new job.
   a Thanks. Have a nice weekend.
   b Thanks. I'm going to miss you.
5 Thanks for everything.
   a Sorry.
   b You're welcome.

13 Put the conversation in the correct order.

A: We're going to miss you. All the best.   ____
A: This is for you, from everybody.   *1*
A: You're welcome.   ____
B: Thanks for everything. Goodbye, everybody.   ____
B: Thanks.   ____

Writing
Signing off

14 Choose the correct alternative to complete the sentences.

1 See *you* / *us* then.
2 All *the best* / *regards*.
3 Kind *regards* / *love*.
4 Best *wishes* / *love*.
5 Give my *wishes* / *love* to Tom.
6 Yours *regards* / *faithfully*.

15 Use the expressions from exercise 14 to write the endings on the following messages.

1 a social network message to an old friend

> Can you send me new photos of your children?
> *Give my love to Tom*
> Love F xx

2 a message on a leaving card

> *Good luck in your new job.*
> _____
> *Kim xx*

3 a text message to good friend

> Yes, 6.00 p.m. tomorrow.
> _____
> P

4 a business letter

> _____
> James White
> Head of Marketing

5 a message to someone you don't know very well

> *Thank you very much for the flowers.*
> _____
> *Fadila*

Audio script

UNIT 1 RECORDING 1

1: Hello, I'm Roy McGee.
2: Are you Theresa Daly?
3: Hello, what's your name?
4: A: Hello, my name's Frank.
  B: Hi, I'm Paola. Nice to meet you.

UNIT 1 RECORDING 2

Conversation 1
A: Hello, I'm Nina.
B: Hi, Nina. My name's Florian.
Conversation 2
A: Are you Judith?
B: Yes, that's right.
Conversation 3
A: Hello, I'm Simon. What's your name?
B: My name's Jonathan. Nice to meet you.

UNIT 1 RECORDING 3

1 My name's Jean.
2 I'm Bruno.
3 Hello, I'm Patricia.
4 Is your name Suzanne?
5 Are you Asif?
6 What's your name?

UNIT 1 RECORDING 4

1 **act**or
2 **tea**cher
3 **assis**tant
4 po**lice**
5 ac**coun**tant
6 **bus**iness
7 engi**neer**
8 **wai**ter

UNIT 1 RECORDING 5

1 C, a, t, h, e, r, i, n, e. Z, e, t, a. J, o, n, e, s. Catherine Zeta-Jones.
2 J, u, l, i, e, t. B, i, n, o, c, h, e. Juliet Binoche.
3 Q, u, e, n, t, i, n. T, a, r, a, n, t, i, n, o. Quentin Tarantino.
4 K, e, v, i, n. S, p, a, c, e, y. Kevin Spacey.

UNIT 1 RECORDING 6

1 Hello. My name's Sophia and my surname is Spencer.
  It's spelt S-P-E-N-C-E-R. I'm an actor. My email address is
  sspencer@yahoo.com.
2 Hi. My name's Tony. My family name is Banbury. That's B-A-N-B-U-R-Y.
  My phone number is 07963 241856. I'm an engineer.

UNIT 1 RECORDING 7

Mala: Hello, I'm Mala. What's your name?
Lorenzo: Hi, Mala. My name's Lorenzo. Nice to meet you.
Mala: Nice to meet you, too. How do you spell your name?
Lorenzo: L – O – R – E – N – Z – O.
Mala: Lorenzo, this is Louis.
Lorenzo: Hi, Louis. Nice to meet you.
Mala: Goodbye, Lorenzo. See you again.
Lorenzo: Goodbye, Mala.

UNIT 1 RECORDING 8

1 I
2 I'm
3 Hi!
4 fine
5 nice
6 my

UNIT 2 RECORDING 1

1 Hello. My name's Adam.
2 I'm Francesca. Nice to meet you.
3 Where are you from?
4 I'm from Italy.
5 Are you from Rome?
6 No, I'm from Milan.
7 Are you a student?
8 No, I'm your teacher.

UNIT 2 RECORDING 2

1 **A:** Is Miles a waiter?
  B: No, he's an actor.
2 **A:** Is Bruno from Brazil?
  B: Yes, he is.
3 **A:** Is Paula from Italy?
  B: Yes, she is.
4 **A:** Is Yasmin a teacher?
  B: No, she isn't. She's a student.
5 **A:** Is her name Mary?
  B: No, it's Maria.
6 **A:** Is Hanoi in Vietnam?
  B: Yes, it is.
7 **A:** Is his name Giles?
  B: Yes, it is.
8 **A:** Is Perth in the USA?
  B: No, it's in Australia.

UNIT 2 RECORDING 3

1 He's from Britain. He's British.
2 She's from the United States. She's American.
3 He's from Japan. He's Japanese.
4 She's from China. She's Chinese.
5 He's from Brazil. He's Brazilian.
6 She's from Portugal. She's Portuguese.
7 She's from Egypt. She's Egyptian.
8 He's from Argentina. He's Argentinian.

UNIT 2 RECORDING 4

1 She's American.
2 His first name's Juan.
3 What's his name?
4 Her surname's Bell.
5 He's Portuguese.
6 She's from China.
7 Where's he from?
8 What's her name?

UNIT 2 RECORDING 5

What is Yale and where is it?
Yale is a university in the United States of America – the USA. It's in New Haven, Connecticut.

What are the UK and the UAE?
The UK is the United Kingdom – England, Scotland, Wales and Northern Ireland. London is the capital city of the United Kingdom. The UAE is the United Arab Emirates – seven countries in the Persian Gulf. The capital is Abu Dhabi.

What is Machu Picchu and where is it?
Machu Picchu is an old city in the Urubamba Valley in Peru, in South America.

Where is New South Wales? Is it in Wales?
No! New South Wales isn't in Wales ... and it isn't in the United Kingdom. It's in Australia. The capital is Sydney.

Where is the Taj Mahal? How old is it?
The Taj Mahal is in Agra, a city in India. It's about four hundred years old.

UNIT 3 RECORDING 1

1 places
2 sandwich
3 student
4 nationalities
5 addresses
6 country
7 children
8 people
9 woman
10 men

UNIT 3 RECORDING 2

1 'Is this your pen?'
2 'Are those people from Japan?'
3 'Who's that in the café?' 'My teacher.'
4 'What are these?' 'I don't know.'
5 'Is this your car?' 'Yes, it is.'
6 'Who are those children over there?'
7 'Is that hotel expensive?' 'Yes, it is!'

UNIT 3 RECORDING 3

1 Is the shop expensive?
   - No, it's cheap.
2 Is he friendly?
   - No, he's very unfriendly.
3 Is Ali happy?
   - No, he's sad.
4 Isn't this fantastic?
   - No, it's awful.

UNIT 3 RECORDING 4

Places to eat in Newcastle

The Sushiya is a Japanese restaurant. It's in the city centre. The food is fantastic, but it isn't cheap. The waiters are very friendly. It's a great restaurant! Five stars!

The new Italian restaurant, *The Piccolo*, is expensive and the food is awful. The waiters are English, not Italian. They are unfriendly. This is not my favourite restaurant! One star.

The Argentinian restaurant, *Vaqueros*, isn't in the city centre, but it is cheap and the food is great. The waiters are from Buenos Aires and very friendly. I like it! Four stars.

The Chinatown is a Chinese restaurant. It is cheap, but the food isn't fantastic. The waiters are friendly. Two stars.

UNIT 3 RECORDING 5

1 Can I have coffee, please?
2 Eggs for me, please.
3 Can I have a sandwich, please?
4 The same for me, please.
5 Can I have the bill, please?

UNIT 3 RECORDING 6

Waiter: Yes, please?
Customer 1: Can I have a ham sandwich, please?
Waiter: And for you, sir?
Customer 2: Fish for me, please.
Waiter: And to drink?
Customer 1: Can I have coffee, please? Black coffee.
Customer 2: Orange juice for me, please.
Waiter: Anything else?
Customer 2: No, thank you.

UNIT 4 RECORDING 1

1 ca**fé**
2 ho**tel**
3 **sho**pping
4 **res**taurant
5 **cin**ema
6 **sta**tion

UNIT 4 RECORDING 2

1 The bank's in the square.
2 'Where's the station?' 'It's on the left.'
3 The restaurant's on the right.
4 Is your hotel near the station?
5 The cinema is on the left of the restaurant.
6 Is the hotel in Station Road?
7 The cinema isn't in the square.
8 The hotel is on the left of the train station.

UNIT 4 RECORDING 3

1 There's a hotel in Crowley.
2 There are three restaurants.
3 There's an Italian restaurant.
4 There are three cafés.
5 There's a supermarket in Marton Road.
6 There's a cinema in Church Street.
7 There are two car parks.
8 There are two banks in Market Square: *NatWest* and *Barclays*.
9 There's a post office in Park Street.

UNIT 4 RECORDING 4

1 These apples are cheap.
2 Where are they?
3 That man is very friendly.
4 There are three women in the picture.
5 There's a cathedral in the city centre.
6 This restaurant is very expensive.
7 Are those shops good?
8 This is my favourite hotel.
9 There's a yellow taxi in the picture.
10 Those men are in a café.

UNIT 4 RECORDING 5

The World Showcase

The World Showcase is in Disney World in Florida, USA. There are eleven pavilions at the beautiful World Showcase Lagoon – and all the pavilions are about a different country in the world.

In the Chinese pavilion, there are two Chinese restaurants. In the Moroccan pavilion, there's a real Moroccan market.

For France, there's the Eiffel Tower (a small one) and there's a cinema.

In the Italian pavilion, there's an Italian restaurant – *Alfredo's* – with real Italian pasta.

And in the United Kingdom pavilion, there's a pub – *The Rose and Crown* – with English food and drinks.

In the Japanese pavilion, there's a Japanese garden and a big Japanese store – *Mitsukoshi*.

UNIT 4 RECORDING 6

1 There isn't a five-star hotel.
2 There aren't any Indian restaurants.
3 There isn't a train station.
4 There aren't any internet cafés.
5 There isn't a library.
6 There aren't any beaches.

Audio script

UNIT 4 RECORDING 7

1 Is there a park?
2 Are there any good shops?
3 Is there a university?
4 Is there a bus station?
5 Are there any cheap bars?
6 Is there a cinema?

UNIT 4 RECORDING 8

Conversation 1
Woman: Excuse me. Where's Park Road?
Man: It's down there ... on the right.
Conversation 2
Man: Excuse me. Is there a bank near here?
Woman: Yes, it's down there, near the supermarket, on the left.
Conversation 3
Man: Excuse me. Is there a café near here?
Woman: Yes, it's in Park Road.
Conversation 4
Woman: Excuse me. Where's the bus station?
Man: It's in Station Road, on the right.
Woman: Thank you.
Man: You're welcome.

UNIT 5 RECORDING 1

1 Antonio is Marta's husband.
2 Marta is Antonio's wife.
3 Their son's name is Javier.
4 Javier is Gloria's brother.
5 Gloria is Javier's sister.
6 Antonio and Marta are Javier and Gloria's parents.
7 Hugo and Elvira are Gloria and Javier's grandparents.
8 Gloria and Javier are Hugo and Elvira's grandchildren.

UNIT 5 RECORDING 2

My name's Carla. My husband's name is Miguel. We have one child, Lotta. She's 18. We're from Spain, but we don't live there now. We live in Ireland. I work in a college near Dublin. I teach Spanish. Miguel and Lotta work in an expensive hotel in the city centre. They study English in the evening. I don't study in the evening – I teach in the evening!

Miguel and Lotta go to work by bus because we live near the college, we don't live in the city centre. We don't live in a house. We have a big flat near a park – it's fantastic. We are very happy here.

UNIT 5 RECORDING 3

1 I study English.
2 I don't study French.
3 They have a big car.
4 They don't have a small car.
5 You work in an office.
6 You don't work in a hotel.
7 We like coffee.
8 We don't like tea.
9 I go to work by bus.
10 I don't go to work by train.
11 They live in Wales.
12 They don't live in Germany.

UNIT 5 RECORDING 4

1 We don't work in an office.
2 They don't go to work by bus.
3 I don't like coffee.
4 You don't study French.
5 We don't have an expensive car.

UNIT 5 RECORDING 5

1 Do you live in a house or a flat?
   I live in a flat.
2 Do you study German?
   No I don't. I study English.
3 Do they have any children?
   Yes, two. Their names are Tom and Anna.
4 Do you live in a town or a city?
   I live in Fermo – it's a town in Italy.
5 Do you have any pets?
   No, I don't like animals.
6 Do you have any brothers and sisters?
   Yes, one brother. His name's Mark.
7 Do you like Chinese food?
   No, I don't. I like Japanese food.
8 Do you work in an office?
   Yes, I do. I'm an accountant.
9 Do you live with your parents?
   No, I don't. I live with a friend.
10 Do Maria and Guiseppe teach Italian or Spanish?
   They teach both – Italian and Spanish!

UNIT 5 RECORDING 6

1 Do you live in a house?
   Yes, I do.
2 Do you study Japanese?
   No, I don't.
3 Do you have any sisters?
   Yes, I do.
4 Do you live in America?
   No, I don't.
5 Do you like dogs?
   Yes, I do.
6 Do you have a dog?
   No, I don't.

UNIT 5 RECORDING 7

1 Do you study French?
2 Do you study at home?
3 Do you live alone?
4 Do you live in a house?
5 Who do you live with?
6 Where do you work?
7 Do you have any children?
8 Do you go to work by car?

UNIT 6 RECORDING 1

1 use
   uses
   uses a computer
   She uses a computer.
2 read
   reads
   reads the newspaper
   He reads the newspaper.
3 listen
   listens
   listens to music
   My friend listens to music.
4 cook
   cooks
   cooks dinner
   My father cooks dinner.

UNIT 6 RECORDING 2

Famous couples

Will Smith is an American actor and rap singer from Philadelphia, USA. He is in the TV series *Fresh Prince of Bel Air*, and in the films *Men in Black* (1996), and *Independence Day* (1997). His wife is actress Jada Pinkett Smith. She is in *The Nutty Professor* with Eddie Murphy, and in the film *Scream 2*. They have two children, Jaden and Willow and they live in Los Angeles.

Iman – her full name is Iman Abdul Marid – is forty seven years old, and she comes from Somalia in Africa. She is a supermodel, an actress and an international businesswoman. She is married to British rock star and actor David Bowie: real name (David Robert Jones). They both have one child from other marriages and they have a daughter, Alexandra Zara Jones. They live in New York.

UNIT 6 RECORDING 3

1
A: Does Will Smith appear in the film *Men in Black*?
B: Yes, he does.
2
A: Where is he from?
B: He's from Philadelphia, USA.
3
A: What is his wife's name?
B: His wife's name is Jada Pinkett Smith.
4
A: What are their children's names?
B: Their children's names are Jaden and Willow.
5
A: Where do Will and Jada live now?
B: They live in Los Angeles.

UNIT 6 RECORDING 4

1
A: How old is Iman?
B: She's forty seven years old.
2
A: Where is she from?
B: She's from Somalia.
3
A: Is she married?
B: Yes she is – to David Bowie.
4
A: Do they have any children?
B: Yes, they have one daughter.
5
A: Where do they live?
B: They live in New York.

UNIT 6 RECORDING 5

1 Does Tina eat meat?
No, she doesn't.
Does Tony eat meat?
Yes, he does.
2 Does Tina drink a lot of coffee?
No, she doesn't.
Does Tony drink a lot of coffee?
Yes, he does.
3 Does Tina like rock music?
No, she doesn't.
Does Tony like rock music?
Yes, he does.
4 Does Tina like dancing?
Yes, she does.
Does Tony like dancing?
No, he doesn't.
5 Does Tina study a foreign language?
Yes, she does.
Does Tony study a foreign language?
No, he doesn't.
6 Does Tina speak French?
Yes, she does.
Does Tony speak French?
No, he doesn't.
7 Does Tina play a sport?
Yes, she does.
Does Tony play a sport?
No, he doesn't.
8 Does Tina like computer games?
No, she doesn't.
Does Tony like computer games?
Yes, he does.

UNIT 6 RECORDING 6

1 Does he ... ?
Does he listen ... ?
Does he listen to music?
2 Does she ... ?
Does she play ... ?
Does she play tennis?

UNIT 6 RECORDING 7

1 I like Chinese food.
2 I love Robbie Williams.
3 I don't like cooking.
4 I don't mind classical music.
5 I hate football.

UNIT 6 RECORDING 8

Conversation 1
A: Would you like a sandwich?
B: No, thanks.
Conversation 2
A: How about a coffee?
B: Yes, please.
Conversation 3
A: How about something to drink?
B: A bottle of water, please.
Conversation 4
A: Would you like some popcorn?
B: Yes, please.
Conversation 5
A: Coffee?
B: White, please.

Audio script

UNIT 6 RECORDING 9

A: Would you like a coffee?
B: Yes, black coffee, please.
A: How about something to eat?
B: No, thanks. I'm OK.
A: Are you sure? How about a chocolate?
B: Well, yes, please. I love chocolates.
A: Here you are.

UNIT 7 RECORDING 1

I get up early, at quarter to six and go to work at about half past six. I have breakfast in a café near my office and start work at half past seven. I don't have a big lunch, just a sandwich and a coffee. I usually finish work at about six o'clock. I get home at seven, then I have dinner with my husband – he loves cooking! After dinner we usually watch TV, then I go to bed early, at about ten o'clock and sleep for seven or eight hours.

UNIT 7 RECORDING 2

1   I sometimes get up early.
2   I don't usually play tennis at the weekend.
3   My brother and I always play football at the weekend.
4   Shops in our town sometimes open at night.
5   Barbara doesn't usually work on Mondays.
6   I usually listen to music when I get home.
7   Children in Britain never go to school on Sundays.
8   We always go to work by train.

UNIT 7 RECORDING 3

Life in Britain today

Food
British people like good food and more than half of them go to a restaurant every month. Fast food is also very popular – 30% of all adults have a burger every three months, but 46% have fish and chips!

Sport
British people don't do a lot of sport. Only 17% of people go swimming every week, 9% go cycling and 8% play golf. Football is the most popular sport in Britain; 10% of the population play it and 46% watch it.

Cinema and TV
Films are very popular in Britain and about 60% of people between 15 and 24 go to the cinema every month. At home, men watch TV for about 28 hours every week – two hours more than women.

Holidays
British people love going on holiday and have 56 million holidays a year. The most popular holiday destinations in the UK are Cornwall, Devon, Somerset, Dorset and the South Coast. British people also like to go abroad on holiday; 27% go to Spain, 10% go to the USA and 9% go to France. Maybe this is because the weather in Britain isn't always very good!

UNIT 7 RECORDING 4

1   a   **Mon**day
    b   Mon**day**
2   a   **Tues**day
    b   Tues**day**
3   a   Wednes**day**
    b   **Wednes**day
4   a   **Thurs**day
    b   Thurs**day**
5   a   **Fri**day
    b   Fri**day**
6   a   Satur**day**
    b   **Satur**day
7   a   **Sun**day
    b   Sun**day**

UNIT 7 RECORDING 5

Interviewer: What's the name of your new film?
Chad: It's called *Blood in the Afternoon*.
Interviewer: When is it in cinemas?
Chad: On Friday.
Interviewer: Why do people like your films?
Chad: Because they're fast and exciting, I think.
Interviewer: Who's your favourite actor?
Chad: I love Robert De Niro – he's great.
Interviewer: Where's your wife from?
Chad: She's from Palermo, in Italy.
Interviewer: How many houses do you have?
Chad: Three, I think – no, four.

UNIT 7 RECORDING 6

1   How many people live in the UK?
2   Where does your brother live?
3   What is the capital of Colombia?
4   Who's your favourite singer?
5   Why do you study English?
6   When do you usually go to the cinema?
7   How many languages does Monica speak?

UNIT 7 RECORDING 7

1   Who's your favourite actress?
2   Where do you work?
3   When do you go to bed?
4   Why do you study English?
5   What do you do in the evening?
6   How many people are there?

UNIT 8 RECORDING 1

AIBO – the electronic pet

What exactly is an AIBO, and why do people love them so much?

An AIBO is a robot dog, about twenty-eight centimetres long and it can do lots of amazing things. For example, it can walk, run, play with a ball, be happy or sad – just like a real dog. It can also dance, sing songs, see colours and take photographs like a camera!

A new (or 'baby') AIBO can't see or hear, but it can understand about forty words and phrases, like *How old are you?*, *Good boy* and *Don't do that*. Say its name and it answers you; say goodnight and it goes to sleep. When it becomes older, the AIBO learns more words and soon it can talk to you, too. And when it's an 'adult' it can check your emails and read them to you.

These robot pets are very popular in Japan and the USA, but they aren't cheap. Each AIBO is about seven thousand, five hundred dollars – so maybe a real dog is better!

UNIT 8 RECORDING 2

1   I can ride a bicycle, but I can't swim.
2   Margie's always late for work because she can't get up early.
3   Their daughter's only six months old, so she can't talk or read.
4   I'm sorry, I can't understand this sentence.
5   I can play chess, but I don't often win!
6   My husband can cook very well. The food he makes is delicious!
7   Joe can speak French and Spanish fluently, but he can't speak Chinese.
8   My sister can play the violin brilliantly.

UNIT 8 RECORDING 3

1 He can drive.
2 She can't swim.
3 He can play chess.
4 They can dance very well.
5 They can't speak Spanish.
6 I can run very fast.
7 I can't read music.
8 She can't ride a bike.
9 He can't play chess.
10 He can remember all his friends' birthdays.

UNIT 8 RECORDING 4

1 Can you dance?
2 Can he swim?
3 Can they play the guitar?
4 Can she ride a bike?
5 Can she swim?
6 Can you drive a car?
7 Can he run fast?
8 Can they cook?

UNIT 8 RECORDING 5

1 A: Can you cook?
   B: Yes, I can.
2 A: Can your parents speak English?
   B: No, they can't.
3 A: Can Jim play football well?
   B: No, he can't.
4 A: Can your daughter read and write?
   B: Yes, she can.
5 A: Can you swim?
   B: No, I can't.
6 A: Can your son read music?
   B: Yes, he can.
7 A: Can your friends play tennis?
   B: Yes, they can.

UNIT 8 RECORDING 6

Woman: Excuse me, can you tell me the time, please?
Man: Yes, of course. It's 12 o'clock.
Woman: Thanks. Can you tell me where the Eiffel Tower is?
Man: Yes, it's on the left bank.
Woman: The left bank? Can I look at your map, please?
Man: Sorry, I don't have one.
Woman: Oh, well, can you take me to the Eiffel Tower, please?
Man: No, I can't. I'm sorry, but I'm late!

UNIT 9 RECORDING 1

1 January
2 February
3 April
4 July
5 August
6 September
7 October
8 November
9 December

UNIT 9 RECORDING 2

1 the 14th of February
2 the 28th of January
3 the 2nd of October
4 the 12th of June
5 the 13th of November
6 the 30th of August
7 the 8th of December
8 the 15th of March
9 the 17th of July
10 the 16th of April
11 the 3rd of May
12 the 26th of September

UNIT 9 RECORDING 3

When they were young
Arnold Schwarzenegger was born in 1947 in a small village near Graz, in Austria. His family was very poor and life in Austria was difficult. He was very good at sports, especially bodybuilding, and in 1972 he was 'Mr Universe'. He 's now a famous Hollywood actor and politician and lives in the United States.

Barrack Obama was born in Honolulu, Hawaii, in 1961. At school he was called 'O Bomber' because he was good at basketball. His first job was in an ice cream shop and now he doesn't like ice cream. Now he's a politician and he became the President of the United States in 2009.

Ricky Martin was born in Puerto Rico, in the Caribbean, in 1971. From the age of twelve to seventeen he was a singer in the Latin-American pop band Menudo. His song, La Copa de la Vida, was the official 1998 Football World Cup song. He's now a famous singer and he can speak five languages fluently!

UNIT 9 RECORDING 4

1 He wasn't very rich.
2 They weren't from Japan.
3 There wasn't a supermarket in the square.
4 Their car wasn't very expensive.
5 Marco's grandmother wasn't French.
6 His parents weren't poor.
7 My brothers weren't at home last night.

UNIT 9 RECORDING 5

My name's Niall Kelly and I was born in 1946, in a village called Mallahyde, in Ireland. My father, Donald, was an engineer and Maeve, my mother, was a nurse. There were six people in our family: my parents, my three sisters and me.

My sisters were usually very noisy, but I was a quiet child. I wasn't happy at my first school. I wasn't good at maths or English, but I was good at sport, especially football.

I remember my best friends were two brothers called Jim and Adam and they weren't good at school, they were always very naughty in class! I also remember my favourite food – it was hot bread!

UNIT 9 RECORDING 6

1 What was his job?
2 Where were they from?
3 Why were you late for class?
4 What was on TV last night?
5 Who were you with yesterday afternoon?
6 Was Michel at school yesterday?
7 What was your grandmother's name?
8 Were both your parents from Russia?

Audio script

UNIT 9 RECORDING 7

1. nineteen forty-two
2. nineteen ninety-nine
3. two thousand and seven
4. eighteen fifty-six
5. two thousand and one
6. eighteen sixty-five

UNIT 10 RECORDING 1

1. My wife lived in Columbia when she was young.
2. Their father died when he was eighty-six.
3. My grandfather worked for a British company.
4. We studied the Past simple in class today.
5. Dylan played computer games all night.
6. Last night, I watched a really good film on TV.
7. Gabriela started her new job two days ago.
8. It was a beautiful day, so I walked to work.

UNIT 10 RECORDING 2

moved	walked	wanted
painted	lived	played
cooked	hated	watched
loved	returned	listened

UNIT 10 RECORDING 3

The Kennedys

John F Kennedy is probably the most famous president in American history, but the story of the Kennedy family is not a happy one.

John was born in Boston, USA in 1917. The Kennedys were a big family and John had five sisters and three brothers. His father, Joseph Kennedy, was a businessman and his mother Rose was the daughter of a politician. After university, John worked as a journalist, then became a politician in 1946. But this was an unhappy time for the Kennedy family – John's brother, Joe died in the Second World War and four years later, his sister, Kathleen died in a plane crash. John became a senator in 1952, the same year he met his wife, Jacqueline Bouvier. They got married in 1953 and had three children – but their third child, Patrick, died two days after he was born. In 1961, John F Kennedy became President and he was very popular with the American people. He died in Dallas, Texas in November 1963 and his brother Bobby also died five years later. The Kennedys are a famous family, but their story is a very sad one.

UNIT 10 RECORDING 4

1. Joanna left home when she was eighteen.
2. Last night, I went to the cinema.
3. They sold their car to a friend's son for two thousand pounds.
4. Alfred Hitchcock made fifty-three films in his life.
5. My parents bought this house when they moved here in 1964.
6. She became an actress after she left school.
7. When we were children, we had a dog.
8. Erica met her husband when she was on holiday.

UNIT 10 RECORDING 5

1. I'm sorry.
2. Thank you very much.
3. That's all right.
4. You're welcome.
5. I'm sorry I'm late.
6. Thank you for the card.
7. So sorry.
8. No problem.
9. That's very kind.
10. Don't worry.

UNIT 11 RECORDING 1

The only way to travel

In 1865, a Belgian man, Georges Nagelmackers, had an idea. He wanted to build a train to travel across Europe and into Asia. Nagelmackers saw Pullman's sleeper cars on the trains in America. Passengers slept on the journey and it was comfortable. Nagelmackers decided to design a train with sleeper cars for Europe. He wanted his train to be fantastic – like a really good hotel inside.

On 4th October, 1883, his train departed from the train station the *Gare de Strasbourg* in Paris. It was called *The Orient Express*. Everybody wanted to travel on *The Orient Express*. Famous passengers were King Ferdinand of Bulgaria, King Leopold the 3rd of Belgium and Czar Nicholas the 2nd of Russia. There were also lots of journalists on the train. The journey went from Paris in France to Istanbul in Turkey and it took four days. The first passengers enjoyed the journey so much that everyone wanted to travel on *The Orient Express*.

You can travel on *The Orient Express* today, but it isn't the original one.

UNIT 11 RECORDING 2

1. Did Stephanie go to the beach?
2. Did Bob go swimming?
3. Were the children happy?
4. Did Bob like the hotel?
5. Was the beach nice?
6. Did Carla and Matthew like the hotel?
7. Did Carla and Matthew go shopping?
8. Was Bob happy?

UNIT 11 RECORDING 3

1. Where did she go to university?
2. When did she get married?
3. When did she become Prime Minister?
4. How many children did she have?
5. When did he start playing the guitar?
6. Where did he go in 1966?
7. How many albums did he make?
8. When did he die?
9. How many brothers and sisters did he have?
10. Where did he live?
11. When did he die?
12. How many books did he write?

UNIT 11 RECORDING 4

1. Were you?
2. Were you happy?
3. Were you tired after work?
4. Were you late?
5. Were you on time?
6. Did you?
7. Did you go?
8. Did you buy a return ticket?
9. Did you have a good journey?
10. Did you go on a train journey?

UNIT 11 RECORDING 5

Railway Employee:	Yes, please?
Customer:	Can I have a ticket to York, please?
Railway Employee:	Single or return?
Customer:	Return, please.
Railway Employee:	That's £33.50.
Customer:	What time's the next train?
Railway Employee:	It's at 16.12.
Customer:	Which platform?
Railway Employee:	Platform 4.
Customer:	Thank you.
Railway Employee:	You're welcome.

UNIT 11 RECORDING 6

Railway Employee:	Yes, please?
Customer:	Can I have a ticket to Liverpool, please?
Railway Employee:	Single or return?
Customer:	Single, please.
Railway Employee:	That's £52.60.
Customer:	What time's the next train?
Railway Employee:	It's at 10.30.
Customer:	Which platform?
Railway Employee:	Platform 3.
Customer:	Thank you.
Railway Employee:	You're welcome.

UNIT 12 RECORDING 1

1 I want to watch TV tonight.
2 Do you want to go shopping?
3 No, I don't.
4 I want to see a film this afternoon.
5 I don't want to go out tomorrow.
6 I want a cup of coffee after the lesson.
7 I don't want to do my homework tonight.
8 Does he want to come to the café?
9 Yes, he does.
10 What do you want to do tomorrow?

UNIT 12 RECORDING 2

1 I want to go on holiday.
2 I don't want to watch TV.
3 I want a new bag.
4 I want to go out tonight.
5 I don't want a new jacket.
6 I want a dog.

UNIT 12 RECORDING 3

1 I'm going to play tennis this weekend.
2 He isn't going to have lunch with his sister.
3 They're going to see the Taj Mahal next week.
4 Chris isn't going to buy a mobile phone.
5 We're going to see a film this evening.
6 I'm going to visit my friend Mark in hospital.
7 Margie and Vanessa aren't going to buy any clothes next weekend.
8 Luca is going to start a new job on Monday.

UNIT 12 RECORDING 4

1 Are you going to phone Jack?
2 What are you going to do tonight?
3 Where are you going to go on holiday?
4 Are your parents going to move house?
5 What's Bob going to study at university?
6 Is she going to study English next year?

UNIT 12 RECORDING 5

1 going to visit
2 Are you going to visit?
3 going to see
4 Are you going to see Jim?
5 going to have
6 I'm going to have breakfast.
7 going to buy
8 They're going to buy a card.
9 going to cook
10 She's going to cook dinner.

UNIT 12 RECORDING 6

Holiday destinations

Paris

Paris, the capital of France, is a great place for a holiday. You can visit famous buildings and museums like the Eiffel Tower and the Louvre. Or you can go shopping along the Champs Élysées and have a drink or a meal in one of the many cafés and restaurants. You can travel along the River Seine by boat or go for a walk in the Luxembourg Gardens, one of the many beautiful parks in the city. Paris is also the home of many famous artists. Picasso, Toulouse Lautrec and Rodin all lived in Paris. So come and stay for a weekend or a month … there's always lots to do in Paris!

Istanbul

The Turkish city of Istanbul is a wonderful place to visit. In the old part of the city there are lots of interesting buildings, like the 500-year-old Topkapi Palace. There are also two beautiful mosques very near the Palace; the Sancta Sophia and the famous Blue Mosque. Most visitors to Istanbul go shopping in the city's biggest market, the 'Grand Bazaar'. There are more than four thousand shops there and you can buy books, food, clothes, flowers and carpets. The food in Istanbul is great and the city has some fantastic fish restaurants. So, come and visit Istanbul – the city where Asia meets Europe!

Hong Kong

You can't visit Hong Kong without shopping! There are many beautiful department stores, boutiques and markets in Hong Kong where you can buy everything from food and clothes to interesting souvenirs. Hong Kong is also great for eating out. There are over 11,000 restaurants in Hong Kong, so you can eat wonderful Chinese food in a different place every day. Hong Kong is a busy place, but there are many parks and other quiet places where you can sit and look at the fantastic views. Come and visit Hong Kong … there's nowhere like it!

Pearson Education Limited
Edinburgh Gate
Harlow
Essex CM20 2JE
England
and Associated Companies throughout the world.

www.pearsonelt.com

First published 2014
Sixth impression 2019
ISBN: 978-1-4479-0670-4 (Cutting Edge Starter New Edition Workbook
with Key)
ISBN: 978-1-4479-0672-8 (Cutting Edge Starter New Edition Workbook
without Key)

Set in 10.5pt Bliss Light
Printed in Slovakia by Neografia

Photo acknowledgements
*The publisher would like to thank the following for their kind permission to
reproduce their photographs:*

(Key: b-bottom; c-centre; l-left; r-right; t-top)

Alamy Images: Arterra Picture Library 19b, Design Pics Inc 38br,
Michael Doolittle 47/5, Mike Goldwater 6/2, JJM Stock Photography 18
(The Japanese Pavilion), Peter Oliver 24, RTimages 5/2, Helen Sessions
18 (Disney World Resort, Orlando Florida), Jack Sullivan 47/2; **Corbis:**
adoc-photos 45b, Henri Bureau 45t, Stephane Cardinale 6 (4), Andrew
Cowie 38t, Hill Street Studios / Blend Images 5/1, Reuters 45c, Mark Sav-
age 6 (1); **DK Images:** Steve Gorton 6/4; **Fotolia.com:** 40c, Apops 5/5,
Arinahabich 27br, Dekanaryas 23r, Flucas 29b, Goodluz 5/4, Michael Jung
14bl, 23l, Leeyiutung 50br, moonrun 8/9, scaliger 49t, skvoor 8/6, 8/7, 8/8,
8/10, Spaxiax 6/1, Gerhard Wanzenböck 42/1; **Getty Images:** Bloomberg
37tc, Hulton Archive 44, Dimitrios Kambouris 25b, Andrew Rich 11/1;
PhotoDisc: Andrew Ward 35r; **Rex Features:** AG / KEYSTONE USA
38b, Best Shot Factory 13l, Broadimage 25t, Courtesy Everett Collection
41, Norbert Kesten 6 (2), Picture Perfect 6 (3), 37tl, Sipa Press 32, 47/6,
Richard Sowersby 47/4, Startraks Photo 37tr; **Robert Harding World
Imagery:** Mel Longhurst 18 (Rose & Crown Pub); **Shutterstock.com:**
Andresr 49tl, Andrey Arkusha 40t, AVAVA 5/6, Gerardo Borbolla 14t, Paul
Brighton 13b, CandyBox Images 31b, ChameleonsEye 19t, Darios 46b,
Dragon Images 35bl, Ros Drinkwater 47/1, Fototaras 47/8, Franco's photos
35t, Giideon 40b, Rostislav Glinsky 47/7, Mandy Godbehear 36, Goodluz
42/6, 46t, Nanette Grebe 42/4, Jorg Hackemann 18 (Town in USA), Mi-
chael Jung 28r, Dmitry Kalinovsky 5/3, 27tl, Alexander Kirch 42/8, Robert
Kneschke 6/6, Michal Kowalski 15, Giancarlo Liguori 50bl, Littleny 21tr,
Viacheslav Lopatin 50t, Lumina Images 5/7, 7tr, Maazur 11/6, Maraze 13t,
Anastasiia Markus 39, Marutti 6/5, MJTH 21bl, Monkey Business Images
51, ndoeljindoel 5/8, 7bl, oliveromg 6/3, 22, Ollyy 42/2, Anton Oparin 30,
Ostill 47/3, Pixel Bliss 29t, Pyty 11/3, Cheryl Savan 31t, Nomad Soul 42/7,
stockcreations 13cr, StockLite 28l, Stockyimages 42/3, Mila Supinskaya
42/5, Syda Productions 27bl, Tobik 13cl, Claudia Veja 43; **SuperStock:**
JJB Photo 9

Cover images: *Front:* **SuperStock:** Don Paulson Photography

All other images © Pearson Education

Every effort has been made to trace the copyright holders and we apologise
in advance for any unintentional omissions. We would be pleased to insert
the appropriate acknowledgement in any subsequent edition of this publica-
tion.

Illustrated by Jeff Anderson (Pennant Inc.), Gary Andrews, Andy Ham-
mond, Kes Hankin (Gemini Design), Connie Jude, Chris Pavely, Mark
Vallance (Gemini Design)